The Forgiveness Solution:

A Step by Step Process to Let it Go

Reverend Misty Tyme

Rev. Misty

Dr. V.

Much love
and thank you
for caring so
much for us!

THE

A STEP BY STEP PROCESS

FORGIVENESS

TO LET IT GO

SOLUTION

REV. MISTY TYME

Sacred Stories
PUBLISHING

Books may be purchased through booksellers or by contacting Sacred Stories Publishing.

The Forgiveness Solution: A Step by Step Process to Let It Go
Reverend Misty Tyme
Graphic Designer: Michelle Wintersteen

Tradepaper ISBN: 978-1-945026-36-2
Electronic ISBN: 978-1-945026-37-9

Library of Congress Control Number:
2017942211

Published by Sacred Stories Publishing
Delray Beach, FL
sacredstoriespublishing.com

Printed in the United States of America

Sacred Stories
PUBLISHING

Dedicated to my twin brother, John Glenn

Acknowledgments

It has been a long road from idea to manuscript. I would like to express my gratitude to all the people who have loving supported me through this book. There are not enough words to express my appreciation.

I would like to thank my publisher Patricia Cagganello, for her support and her passion for bringing divine voices to the world. I would also like to thank my talented graphic designer Michelle Wintersteen. You brought a burst of color to my creation. Thanks to Jessica, Elizabeth, Dan, Cyndie, Helen, Giesla, Chaplin Marilyn, Rev. Swami Omkara, and Rev. Laurie for your author support. To my One Spirit Interfaith Seminary family, I want to thank you for expanding my love of God. Last but far from least, I would like to thank my loving husband, friends and family for supporting me through my own forgiveness story.

TABLE OF CONTENTS

SECTION 1

SECTION 2

REV. MISTY'S FORGIVENESS ALGORITHM™

CONSTRUCT
ESTABLISH YOUR FOUNDATION

Person, Place, or Thing?

Who? What? When? How?

EXAMINE
UNCOVER THE REALITIES

Identify expectations or wishes of the person or situation.

Accurate story is the foundation.

Are you regretful for any of your actions?

Do you need to make apologies or make amends?

Would it help the situation if you did?

PREPARE
FIND SUPPORT AND STRENGTH

Are you ready?

TOOLBOX

Therapy Journaling Spiritual Guidance Prayer Meditation

Reading Dialogue Ceremony Time

FORGIVE
FORGIVENESS IS YOUR CHOICE

Do you choose to have happiness and peace in your heart and mind?
Do you choose to stop trying to control a situation and the people in it?
Do you choose to take responsibility for any hurt you caused through your words, actions, or expectations of others?
Do you choose to have healthy relationships and habits in your life?

Are you ready?

CELEBRATE
EVERYDAY LIFE LIVED WITH FORGIVENESS

The choice of forgiveness gives you a new path in problem solving.
The choice of forgiveness gives your life space for joy.
The choice of forgiveness lets you be more sensitive of your expectations of others and yourself.
The choice of forgiveness lets you see the blessings of an imperfect life.
The choice to forgive reminds each of us that we are in need of forgiveness.

INTRODUCTION
CHAPTER ONE

I am going to go out on a limb here; you picked up this book because you want to work on forgiveness.

Congratulations on being a human with real issues, like the rest of us. Forgiveness can be very hard. The ugly feelings of un-forgiveness come in all types of situations and relationships. They can range from small misunderstandings to threatening and abusive behaviors. It may be psychological, physical, sexual, or financial. Whatever your situation is, you want to get to a solution.

As the title suggests, this is a book about forgiveness. Not just information on what forgiveness is, but the **how** to forgive. Every culture faces the challenge of dealing with forgiveness. All major religions and societies agree forgiveness is a good idea, but both have left out the **how**. *Rev. Misty's Forgiveness Algorithm™* (Forgiveness Algorithm) gives you the **how** and puts it into a step-by-step formula.

The Forgiveness Algorithm came out of my own forgiveness journey. I will share not only my story but also other life-changing forgiveness stories. Laughter opens your heart when so often sadness can slam it tightly shut. I hope to touch your heart and make you smile. In some of the stories, names and places have been changed to protect privacy.

I speak about God and faith in this book. Hey, I am a Reverend! God is big in my life and my belief system. If you choose to call God by another name, that is okay with me. It is your personal relationship. For this book, I will use God or the Divine.

This book is divided into two sections. The first section is to help you see how and why you hold certain forgiveness beliefs. I have also included information on how our society and major religions view forgiveness. The second section is where you get to work on your own forgiveness journey. I have provided pages for you to write your story and answer Work It Questions.

What is the Forgiveness Algorithm?

The result of my forgiveness journey, deep soul searching, and study is the Forgiveness Algorithm. What is an algorithm? An algorithm is simply a problem-solving process. Un-forgiveness is the problem, and this process can help you solve it. It worked for me, my clients and I want it to work for you.

Life is full of complicated people, complicated situations, and complicated decisions. The last thing you need is a complicated way to forgive them. It will take more than singing, "Let it Go," at the top of your lungs and skipping happily into the sunset. In order to truly forgive, you will have to do some real mental, emotional, and even physical work. On this journey, you will go through your turmoil as you work the step-by-step Forgiveness Algorithm, and I plan to be right next to you the whole way.

During the process of this book, I am going to be blunt with you. Just like two good friends sitting together having a cup of tea. I'm sharing my experience, my truth, and the Forgiveness Algorithm. I know you are working on your experiences and your truth. Be candid with yourself and honest with the exercises in the book, it will pay huge dividends.

My goal is to save you some time on your journey. We measure time in everything we do. How long we have known someone. How old we are. How long we've been mad at somebody. How long we've loved somebody. How long it has been since someone we loved has died. We do not have a time machine to go back and grab those bygone moments. We cannot change what already happened. Even if we wish it, rub a lamp, light a candle, pray, or throw a tantrum. What is done is done. We can affect our future by working on the feelings that are left from past situations.

Forgiveness can take time, and depending on the situation; it could take a lifetime. Forgiveness might be something you chip away at, slowly. It is important that you keep moving forward. Forgiveness gives a chance to heal.

Why can forgiveness be so difficult? Because we have entrusted our hearts, minds, body, time, money, vows, and often our life to other people. Then these very same people hurt us. It is easy to let a comment or action go if you do not value who it came from. It is far trickier to forgive the person who means something to us or who meant something to us in the past. A bit of magic would be useful in these situations. POOF!

 The pain is gone and the situation is all better. I wish it worked that way. I would be the first to line up for those magic beans.

If you are over the age of twelve, you know that life requires elbow grease and a set of tools to get what you truly want. And if what you want is to feel better, it will require work. If you choose not to work on your forgiveness issue, you will have exactly what you have now. Wishing that the situation was better or different, and you would still have that nagging pain. You will keep wasting your precious moments. So, save yourself some time, and do the heavy lifting that is required to experience freedom from the emotional weight of un-forgiveness.

There are circumstances when each of us needs to forgive, and a time when we all need to be forgiven. We all have done things we are not proud of. We have all been jealous, mean, or spiteful. We all have the ability to give love and kindness, or to be cruel and nasty. When I say cruel, I am not saying you would make an appearance on the 5 o'clock news, but more along the lines of making biting comments about a friend, neighbor, or the irritating in-law.

You might have had a terrible childhood that still haunts you. And maybe you have even repeated the mistakes of your parents. Hurt likes to

3

repeat itself. Generations of alcoholics are not only biological, but also behavioral. Generations of abuse will roll on until it is consciously changed. *We teach each other how to treat each other.* Harsh words, addict rages, and generations of pain cycles are acted out in families every day. You have the power to stop repeating the pain cycle. You can heal. You can start a new cycle. It is a choice, and it starts with forgiving those who hurt you.

There are as many reasons for un-forgiveness as there are people. Forgiveness can be a tough business. People can be very cruel and abusive. Causing hurt to each other so badly that it does not seem possible that they could ever be forgiven. Yet, the downtrodden rise from the ashes, making beauty out of chaos. Learning to forgive so their life will go on being happier and healthier.

Sometimes our mistakes can make us giggle when we realize how stubborn, and at times just plain stupid we are. I occasionally wonder if God finds our human blunders so humorous? I bet God is getting a bit weary after watching us ordinary humans make such slow progress for the last few thousand years. Thank God for grace. We need it.

My Story

In the second half of my life, I finally decided to answer the whisper I have heard in my ear since I was a little girl. I wanted to help other people. I wanted to be of service to God. As the years passed, this whisper had turned into a yell. By the age of 47, I was all in. I began a two-year Interfaith Seminary program. At the same time, my 84-year-old mother's dementia worsened and I became her care provider. She died two years later, two months before my graduation and ordination as an Interfaith reverend.

After my ordination, I thought my work would primarily be with patients in hospice. Before the recent loss of my mother, I had also lost my adopted father, older sister, older brother, and a best friend to cancer. I had previously worked in Pediatric Oncology and Mental Health, and had witnessed a great deal of loss. Because I had survived so much grief, I felt I could help others navigate it. At times, I had friends who referred to me as "the death and dying girl." Many places I went I would end up in conversations about death, dying, and forgiveness. Little did I know that the subject of forgiveness would one day become a theme in my life and my work.

Glenn

This book is dedicated to my brother, Glenn. You are probably guessing that if a book on forgiveness is dedicated to someone, then that person must have taught me – the author – a lot about forgiveness. You guessed right! If I were to list the people whom I needed to forgive, Glenn would be in the top three.

My brother Glenn gave me a lifetime of situations I could use as examples to hold against him. From drunken rages, physical abuse, and pages of lies. He had committed serious offenses towards me, my family, and even himself. What did all these wrongdoings prove? It proved how wrong he was, and how right I was about almost everything. I was disappointed in who he had turned out to be, and embarrassed that he was my brother.

As siblings, our story starts far earlier than most. Our story began in the womb, because my brother was not only my brother, he was my twin brother. Even now, at the age of 50, I am still asked the question "Are you identical twins?" I usually tilt my head and squish up my nose when I answer, "Well, he's a boy and I'm a girl." Truthfully, we could not be more different.

Arriving early and weighing in at just three pounds each, we had a rough beginning. The word, "rough" was a recurring theme in our lives for years to come. We spent months in the hospital trying to grow and stay alive. My brother stopped breathing many times. In 1966, the highest tech answer to help him was to hit his feet. This would cause him to startle and start breathing again. Considering our rough start, it is quite a feat that we did not have any disabilities. For the era we were born into, this was a miracle.

From the time we were babies, we were each other's playmates and best friends. And we were adorable! Glenn was blonde-haired and blue-eyed, while I had darker hair and the same blue eyes. We developed a twin language that sounded like babble, but according to our family we understood each other perfectly. This twin language disappeared as we learned the English language, and our twin bond disappeared when Glenn's language turned abusive.

Glenn was about 11 years old, and he was angry. He would get so angry that he looked like a ripe tomato topped with a mop of blonde hair. I remember him running out of the front door and down a busy street in a blind fury. My Mother ran out the door after him, finally catching him almost a block away. Glenn flailed about in her arms as she dragged him back to the house. That was the beginning of Glenn's life-long rages.

Our childhood was filled with chaos. Our alcoholic biological father left before we were two years old, and he never returned. Our mother remarried quickly. Our new stepfather was an angry, mean man. So mean, that we were not allowed to come out of our room if he was home. Just nine months later, he left. Even at five years old, I felt relief. That was the end of my Mom's fifth marriage.

Soon that stepfather was replaced with another. This time Mom picked a kinder man. Kinder to us, but he and Mom still drank and fought nightly. I grew up knowing that the sound of ice in a glass meant that soon two adults would be sloshed, fighting and unable to be the parents both my brother and I needed.

Glenn and I spent our childhood protecting each other from our alcoholic parents and all the craziness that life produced. We would witness dinner plates full of food fly across the room and enraged parents being physically abusive to each other. On one occasion, that abuse sent our mother to the hospital with a blood clot on her brain the size of a baseball. From her hospital bed, she asked me to find out who my adoptive Dad was seeing, because she knew he had a new girlfriend. Blatant infidelity from both of our parents was common.

When Glenn and I hit our teen years, Glenn developed into the very same person we once hid from. He turned into a raging man who could not be trusted. My friend and ally was gone, replaced by an ogre. Instead of witnessing the physical abuse, I was now a target for it.

Glenn and our adopted father would get into physical fights that would topple over tables and add to our already tumultuous family life. During one of their brawls, Glenn ended up breaking my Dad's ribs in three places. After this, my father officially became fearful of Glenn. Glenn now recognized he had the power to control all of us.

Glenn's temper was legendary in our family. For example, one day when we were about sixteen, Glenn and I were driving to our high school. Glenn was driving our step dad's new silver pickup truck. I said something to make him angry. Glenn looked at me and yelled, "I will kill us both." This was a serious threat and I knew it. Immediately he started to speed down our small town's main road, skipping all the stop signs and traffic lights. He was trying to cause an accident. I did not scream or yell. I knew from experience that would only make things worse. Then just as suddenly as he went into the rage, he stopped the truck. I jumped out and he sped away. I walked the rest of the way to school.

Glenn told me he was going to kill me a few more times over the years, once with a gun and another time when trying to break down a door. Many other times, he came right to the edge; right where I thought I, or a family member, was going to end up dead. This finally prompted my Mother to remove the hunting rifles from our house.

After years of intimidation and violence, all the memories blur together into a deep dark tangle. At times, it is hard to separate one cruel moment from the next. Why did Glenn do all the things he had done? Was it a result of all the abuse we witnessed from our childhood? Or did our premature birth affect him after all? I suspect both.

Glenn and I no longer had that secret twin telepathy or an unsinkable twin sibling bond we had experienced very early in life. When I saw such twins, I would feel a twinge of "gag me with a spoon" jealousy. Glenn and I were more like distant siblings who did not even call each other on our joint birthdays.

Throughout most of my adult life the majority of my friends did not even know that I had a twin brother. The close friends who did know about him, heard stories of a guy who was nothing like me; a person that lived a life I did not agree with. A life filled with alcohol, abuse, and domineering behavior over the people he was supposed to love.

It was no secret in our family that Glenn was difficult. He was not the family member that you wanted to show up to reunions. He lacked basic social etiquette and you could not trust what he would do. Would he drink too much? Would he get angry? Would he get physically abusive? I would remind everybody in our family that he was the bad one and I was the good one. Not that they needed much reminding, as they had each endured their own run-ins with Glenn.

I knew Glenn wanted to have a close relationship with our older siblings and with me. We would all try to let him back into our lives, hoping it would be better. However, his familiar problematic behaviors quickly caused the usual estrangement. A few years would pass by and we would try again, hoping he had changed. He never changed.

Glenn and I had some random encounters, but generally his life went on without me, and mine without him. The only person in our family who did not put restrictions on their life regarding Glenn was our mother. Every family member had their theories about why she would allow someone to yell at her, call her names, and even physically abuse her into her elder years. My theory is an easy one; this is what our mother was used to. Our mother had six marriages, all physically abusive. Having her son yell at her, threaten her, and use his physical strength to intimidate her, was normal in her world. Our mother was also known for her very intense personality and controlling ways. Glenn and our mother were two peas in an abusive pod.

From a young age, I had expectations that my twin brother would be my lifelong best friend, that he would be even closer than an average brother. I have spent hours wondering what his life, our lives, would have been like if our childhood had been different. I blamed Glenn for not rising above, for not being a better person. The fantasy of Glenn being the twin brother that was supportive, loving, healthy, and happy was never going to happen. My twin brother was an alcoholic and a rage-aholic. I spent thirty-five years smoldering with resentment over the things he had done, and the person he had turned out not to be. I was holding on tightly to my lifelong un-forgiveness.

And then he died.

I was stunned when I received the call. Even though the ambulance was on the way, it was too late; he was gone. Shouldn't I have felt some cosmic connection being cut when he died? Our lives started together in the most connected way. I had absolutely no idea he had left the planet.

Nevertheless, I was not surprised that he had died; he was hardly the portrait of health. Glenn was a short, 49-year-old Swedish man, with skinny legs and a flat butt. He was always in dirty fish-stained Levis with keys attached to a chain jingling out of his pocket. Glenn had a large beer-belly that easily looked like he was smuggling a basketball. He wore his wire-rimmed glasses slightly crooked, and a scent of chewing tobacco wafted from his mouth every time he spoke. Covering his full head of Swedish blonde hair was a baseball hat, which always had some local fishing company's name on it. (I was always a bit envious that he had gotten the blonde hair).

Glenn had done some very violent things during his life; I was surprised he did not end up in prison or dead from a brawl. Glenn had the ability to only pick a fight with those he felt he could win against, and this included women and children.

Before you think my twin brother was a total screw up, I want to let you know that he was also a great chef, he could build anything, and pilot any boat. He was also an extremely hard worker. He volunteered every month to cook a community breakfast at the senior center, and he would fix the roofs of underprivileged neighbors. He checked on the elderly fishermen weekly to talk about the last fishing runs and the newest boat accessory.

When he died, Glenn was in extreme back pain, and he felt out of options. He had suffered with back pain for more than twenty years. Back pain was something he and I shared. The difference was, I had undergone surgery and had followed all the doctor's instructions to fix my broken back. Glenn suffered from an advanced degenerative spine condition that involves the gradual loss of normal structure and function of the spine. He had seen many doctors, searching for a surgical repair or a magic pill to make all his suffering go away. Every surgeon told him that there was no surgical option. What he needed was to take care of himself. Go to physical therapy and stop trying to work like he was a 20-year-old.

Glenn would not stop doing the physical work he loved. Glenn did not regard any of the doctors' advice. He used the term 'physical terrorist' to describe a physical therapist. Glenn refused to slow down, and he continued to use powerful medication to try to mask his symptoms.

I had witnessed one of his painful, debilitating back spasms, which involved his whole back powerfully stiffening. I could see the forcible tightening spread over him, and it sent him to the floor. After each attack, he ended up in bed for days trying not to move, which would only set off another spasm. I still blamed him for not getting better. He wasn't trying hard enough in my opinion. The last time I saw him, he told me that he had found a surgeon who he knew would fix him. I told him to call me after his appointment and let me know what they said. He never called. What I know now is that this surgeon was just another on the long list of doctors who told him that surgery was not an option, that he needed to go to physical therapy, and slow down.

The night he died he was in bed and in terrible pain. He had taken his pain pills and muscle relaxers, but he still had no relief. Glenn told his wife of 25 years that he wanted to die because he was in so much pain and he felt like a burden. He had been in this place many times before, and his wife did not think this one would be any different. After reassuring him that he was not a burden and that she loved him, she slipped into the kitchen to do her nightly chores. She had no idea that was when Glenn decided to *consume all of his pain pills and muscle relaxers. When his wife returned, she thought he had finally fallen asleep.*

Sometime in the night, he died. Glenn's body had suffered from his life of addictions, and could not handle any more. Did Glenn mean to kill himself? Or was he just so desperate to have the pain stop? We will never know. My gut says he did not want to die. Does it really matter? Sometimes it does, but mostly it just makes me very sad. Glenn's pain was both physical and mental. He had a lifetime of anguish caused by the hands of others and his own unhealthy decisions.

At Glenn's funeral, I told stories of us as cute little twins. I told stories of a time when we were friends. The funeral was filled with his children and grandchildren, some salty old fishermen, and a few elderly neighbors. All told stories of Glenn helping them. No one spoke about his demons or the pain he lived in. There were a few comments on his stubborn personality, which brought a knowing laugh from the mourners.

Everyone at the service knew I was his twin sister. It turns out he loved to tell everybody that he was a twin. He was always proud to be my twin, even when I was not proud that he was mine.

Glenn was gone, so what did that mean for me? Was I supposed to only remember the good side of his difficult personality? Would all the damaging and destructive memories disappear because he was dead? How was I going to forgive my brother without him acknowledging he was wrong? After all, he did not live up to my expectations of what a brother should be. Even though he was dead, I stayed angry. I was still deeply rooted in all of the pain and suffering he caused. Yes, he was gone, but all of the bad things that happened to me were not. The pain and anger I carried was still alive and well in me.

*That's when I decided to go back to the beginning of my story. I needed to discover the truth about forgiveness. I needed to find out "**HOW**" to forgive. I wanted to forgive so I could let go of my deep anger and disappointment. I needed to somehow forgive myself for the bitter and uncaring ways I reacted to my brother.*

So, I will tell Glenn's story, our story. I will honor him by not telling every gory detail of his life, because you will miss the part of him that was human. What you should not miss is that forgiveness has allowed me to see our story differently and change my perspective. Forgiveness has allowed me to heal, and I want the same for you.

As you work the Forgiveness Algorithm for your story, please remember that I understand the deep pain that comes from the disappointment of unfulfilled expectations in relationships. That love, no matter how much we want it to solve everything, doesn't fix everything. Forgiveness can be the missing link you need to heal.

FORGIVENESS IS
THE LINK BETWEEN
LOVE AND HEALING

YOUR THOUGHTS:

THE FORGIVENESS QUIZ
CHAPTER TWO

Now is a good time to introduce my forgiveness quiz. It will give you an idea about your current thoughts and feelings about the topic of forgiveness. Do not worry, it is a breeze!

Forgiveness Quiz

Do you think forgiveness is essential to our human experience?
A. No, forgiveness is a myth. I tend to just disregard the situation.
B. Yes, forgiveness is something we all must do and it is important to have a healthy life.
C. Maybe, but only if people are sorry for the pain they have caused and they change their behavior.
D. You get what you give. If you have broken my trust then you should not be in my life.

When someone has hurt you do you expect an apology?
A. Apologies are rare. Most people do not own up to what they have done.
B. No, I don't think people should say they are sorry. It's a bonus if they do.
C. Sure, an apology is great, but I will find it hard to ever trust them again.
D. Yes, they should try to change their behavior and not repeat it.

Do you feel people are out for themselves?

A. Yes! People try to get what they can. People are very self-centered. They want to know, "What have you done for me lately?"

B. No, people make decisions and have beliefs based on their own life experience. Generally, people want to help others.

C. Our society has created greedy people. Everyone is trying to get something or sell you something. If you fall for it, it is your fault.

D. Generally, people think about themselves and that makes it hard to believe they did not know what they were doing.

Forgiveness is important in all major religions. Do you think you are required to forgive?

A. Maybe – forgiveness is okay in some situations, but not if a person does something immoral or illegal.

B. Yes, it is a requirement of God. If God is going to forgive us then we must forgive others.

C. No, religion has it all wrong. You need to get what you give.

D. Religion is too easy on people. I cannot forget what the person did and let them back into my heart only to hurt me all over again.

What is forgiveness to you?

A. Forgiveness is letting go and moving on. This only happens in movies and fairy tales.

B. Forgiveness is letting go of the pain and anger caused by a person or a situation.

C. Forgiveness is letting go of the situation, but remembering the person has shown you who they are. I cannot fix them, but karma will pay them back.

D. Forgiveness can happen sometimes, but trust is hard to earn back.

If you disagree with someone, you...

A. Would give them the correct information because they are misinformed.

B. Would try to see their point of view and not hold it against them if they do not agree with you.

C. Would try to educate them on the issue. If they still do not agree, I agree to disagree. But I am not going to talk to them about the subject again.

D. There is no changing their opinion. They are irrational and too difficult to have in my life.

If you have caused someone pain by your words when you have argued you...

- A. Rarely, I apologize. It takes two to argue, and it is clear that we will not agree.
- B. I would humbly apologize and try to make things right.
- C. I would apologize if I think I was wrong, but making sure the person understands I was in a tough situation.
- D. I might apologize. It depends on the person and if I respect them.

If someone does something illegal or immoral...

- A. Throw the book at them! There are laws for a reason and society should just be done with them.
- B. I understand that they are subject to social justice.
- C. I might forgive them if I can find out why they did what they did and then they apologize. And they never do it again.
- D. People know when they are doing something illegal or immoral. It is not a secret that there are rules in life.

Score

Be conscious that we are all of these things at one time or another. But when dealing with our pain, we usually lean more one way than the other. We have all heard people say things like: "I hope they get what they deserve;" "I would never be able to forgive someone who hurt my family;" "I will never talk to that person again;" "It is easier to not deal with it, because people do not change;" and so on. All of these and a thousand more are common in our culture. We may not even realize we are struggling with un-forgiveness.

When you hear about people forgiving cheating spouses, murderers, and neglectful parents it can leave you thinking that they are some type of special "super forgiver," or they are just stupid. They are not better than you nor are they reckless. They merely understand the power that forgiveness gives them. These people understand what forgiveness is and what it is not.

Count how many A, B, C, or D's you marked. Refer to the descriptions below. Remember we are all the types, but usually we are more one or two of them.

NUMBER OF A's _____ B's _____ C,'s_____ D's_____

If you scored high in the A's you are The Stuffer Non-Forgiver.

If you scored high in the B's you are a Roll off the Duck's Back Forgiver.

If you scored high in the C's you are a Revenge is Sweet Non-Forgiver.

If you scored higher in the D's you are a Once and You're Done Non-Forgiver.

The Stuffer Non-Forgiver

For you, deep forgiveness is a myth. It is like a unicorn. It sounds good and magical, but in real life it is not possible. In your experience, it is unreasonable for you to forgive someone for what they did. You stuff down your un-forgiveness. You will show up at the family reunion, but you won't like it. If someone apologizes, you are okay with it, but you are not going to believe they really mean it. Sure, you can let little things go. But if someone causes pain to you or your loved ones, you cannot forgive them.

Shocker! Many people are exactly like you. Forgiveness is something they do not want to deal with. It is easier to just stuff the situation down and try to forget it. The last thing you need is more conflict. So, you show up, put on a fake smile, and secretly judge the person from afar. You might even understand that people are on their own path, but you do not have to forgive them for it.

Stuffing things down and not dealing with them results in one becoming a last-minute forgiver. This is a common issue in hospice care. Deep family problems, personal regrets, or anger can come bubbling to the surface when faced with the sudden review of your life. If you are lucky, you will be able to resolve and forgive. If not, you will leave behind a legacy of un-forgiveness.

The Roll Off the Duck's Back Forgiver

First I can tell you that you are a rare duck! It is unusual that people can let things go and forgive as easily as you can. The world needs more people like you, who can let things roll off their backs. It is human nature to want a bit of revenge or to not deal with the person at all. But not you! Whether it is just in your DNA, or you have done a lot of work to understand what forgiveness is or is not, you deserve a great big pat on your back.

You can take responsibility for your part in the situation and humbly apologize for the pain you have caused. Way to go.

Forgiveness is a great tool when you have learned to master it. Remember even people that are good forgivers can pick up un-forgiveness. It is important that you check yourself when you feel those ugly feelings.

The Revenge is Sweet Non-Forgiver

Oh yes, it is really sweet, or is it? You are probably saying that you are not a revengeful person. You do not plot and plan in order to cause another person harm. Well, I have a surprise for you! We all do this to some degree. How many times have you thought or said that someone needs to learn his or her lesson? So, you don't call them back, go to dinner with them, or pick them up, because you decided you would teach them a lesson. By trying to teach someone a lesson you are really saying, "I am right and you are wrong, and you deserve what you get." Yes, they might be the worst person ever, but if you decide to treat them badly, what does that say about you? Two wrongs don't make a right, right?

It's understandable to want the person or persons to get a taste of the pain they have caused you. You want to be heard and understood. And you want payback. Somehow in our human brains, we have decided the eye-for-an-eye philosophy will make us feel better and teach the offender a lesson. Usually, an eye-for-an-eye only causes both people to be blind.

The idea that people must pay for what they have done is not necessarily a bad thing, as long as it is not revengeful. If a murderer goes to jail, that is because our society has rules that must be followed to have a healthy, safe society. To send someone to jail for the crime is appropriate, but to wish that they were beaten or murdered in prison, is vengeful. If the offense is less than murder and you think the person is unhealthy, abusive, dangerous, or really irritating, it is not revenge to have healthy boundaries.

The Once and You're Done Non-Forgiver

If you are a Once and You're Done type, you are very protective of your heart. If people do something to you that you feel is wrong, immoral, or criminal, you can never trust them again. Sometimes you do not even bother telling them why you do not want them in your life. You like your life less complicated. It is easier to just be done with the people who hurt you.

Life is full of difficult people with chaotic lives. If you cut all of the difficult people out of your life, you won't have many people left. We all mess up, some more than others, and to different degrees. Yes, you can have healthy boundaries from negative people and situations without slicing all of them out of your life. We all deserve second chances!

Next time you are ready to shut someone out of your life, ask yourself if you are only doing this because it is easier and because you are protecting yourself from further pain. Examine the situation more closely. The relationship with this person might be worth saving.

A Once and You're Done Non-Forgiver will throw away people without ever giving them a chance to make amends. If the person is someone who has hurt you, you will still carry the pain even if you have tossed them away.

18

Applying the Results

The results of the quiz are intended to help you better understand how you approach and manage forgiveness in your life. It is not to say that you can't change over time, but more important that you think about your inner feelings and current frame of mind as it relates to forgiveness and your personality.

YOUR THOUGHTS:

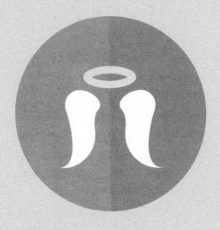

FORGIVENESS IN SOCIETY & RELIGION

CHAPTER THREE

Forgiveness in Society

Let's look at how mainstream society views forgiveness. The Fetzer Institute, a very creative and imaginative place, was established from a desire to help improve the human condition by increasing conscious awareness of the relationship between our inner and outer life. In simpler terms, they study love, forgiveness, and compassion in our lives. The Fetzer Institute is based in Kalamazoo, Michigan but it reaches out to all corners of the world. The Fetzer Institute embraces love as the guiding principle to all of their work.

In 2010, The Fetzer Institute did a survey focused on love and forgiveness. The survey had 1,000 participants, all over the age of 18. According to the survey, "62% of Americans agree (strongly or somewhat) that they need more forgiveness in their personal lives, and this number increases to 83% in their communities, 90% in America, and 90% in the world." It looks like Americans want to forgive and be forgiven. We are not as revenge seeking as we are all made out to be. Or are we? The data went deeper considering what Americans would and would not forgive. This is where things get muddy. This is where you and I are not alone, as many people struggle with forgiveness.

> "67% of Americans agree that the US population is composed of generally forgiving people, but 58% also agree that there are instances where people should never be forgiven. The unforgivable examples are murder (41%), abuse or sexual crimes (26%), or any intentionally committed crime (22%), suggesting that most Americans focus on crimes against an individual as being unforgivable. Additionally, 60% of Americans believe that forgiving someone would first depend on the offender apologizing and making changes."
> (Fetzer Institute, 2010)

The data is suggesting that forgiveness happens only when the other person makes changes or apologizes. Another way to say this is, "I'm right and you're wrong."

The idea that someone is right or wrong defies the logic of forgiveness. Forgiveness is about you letting go of the offense so that you can move forward. A great apology and knowing you are standing on righteous ground helps, but how often are you going to be 100% right? How often will someone give you an apology? Learning to forgive and move forward without someone saying, "I'm sorry," or, "you're right," is a key component to forgiveness.

According to the Fetzer survey, yes, society has begun to realize the importance of forgiveness outside of a religious setting. We want to forgive in our personal life and we want to forgive in society. Even if society has been deceived on what is needed in order to forgive.

Examples where forgiveness is working in our society are programs like Restorative Justice, and victim mediation programs in our prison system. There are 290 victim-offender programs in the United States. Currently the United States has the highest prison population in the world. Criminals and victims rarely meet outside of a courtroom, but that is changing.

A documentary film, "Unlikely Friends" released in 2013 highlights the stories of victims of violent and brutal crimes who forgave their perpetrators. Throughout the movie a common theme arises, the victim forgives the offender so they would no longer be imprisoned by their hurt and anger. They had to unlock the prison doors for themselves and learn that forgiveness is a hard process. However, it doesn't excuse the person for the wrong they did. Even more remarkable, the film goes deeper and shows how the victims befriended the perpetrator. In turn, providing a space for the perpetrator to express their sense of regret and seek forgiveness.

Alcoholics Anonymous

Alcoholics Anonymous (AA) is deeply rooted in our culture. The program started out with a component of spirituality, but you can find many programs that choose not to add this. Most 12 step programs for addiction, from sex addiction (S.A.) to narcotic addiction (N.A.), use a similar outline. Two of the twelve steps deal with forgiveness. One of the steps deals with acknowledging and trying to make amends to those you have hurt. The other is for you to forgive those who have hurt you.

The original Alcoholics Anonymous (AA) was founded in 1934 by Bill Wilson and Dr. Robert Smith, both of whom were alcoholics. The program consists of 12 steps to recovery and is a spiritual based program, but avoids aligning with any specific religious group. AA believes in personal recovery that prescribes to principles over personality. Sober alcoholics that have gone through the 12 steps to recovery help other alcoholics get and stay sober. The program understands that addiction is a progressive multifaceted disease and requires ongoing support. In AA, forgiveness is a powerful tool in rebuilding the life of the alcoholic.

Addicts use the pain and anger of their resentments towards others and themselves as fuel for their addiction, resulting in a circle of pain, resentment, and unhealthy conduct towards the people in their life and themselves. All this pain gets drowned in numbing alcohol.

The eighth and ninth step of AA requires that the alcoholic work on the relationships in their life. Step eight starts the forgiveness journey by writing down a list of names of the people that the alcoholic has hurt. The AA program understands that you must look back to move forward. Working the eighth step lets the alcoholic take an honest look at their motives and actions. This involves forgiving those who have hurt them and trying to make apologies to the people they have hurt. As the alcoholic works through the list of names, they are encouraged to make amends when possible.

"Step Eight: Make a list of all persons we had harmed, and became willing to make amends to them all.

Step Nine: Make direct amends to such people wherever possible, except when to do so would injure them or others."

The following is a story about the power of forgiveness and the influence of Alcoholics Anonymous.

Lisa's Story

I can't remember exactly when I picked up my first drink, but I believe I was about fourteen. My first drink turned into my first experience being drunk. I was a freshman in high school and on a trip with my friends. I also started smoking marijuana and liked that even more than drinking.

It is not unusual for teenagers to start drinking or smoking marijuana, and most of the time they grow out of their party ways. However, I didn't, and eventually drinking took over my life. I remember wishing I would die. Drinking enabled me to stuff my childhood emotional pain so far down in my soul that I did not have to deal with it. I no longer had to feel the pain of abandonment or molestation.

In my later years, drinking threatened my life. Drinking threatened the relationships with my friends and family in ways I could never have foreseen.

When my life was falling apart, I started seeing a therapist. I wanted to know why my drinking had such a hold on me. I wanted to know, "Why did I drink?" In therapy, what I had buried for so long came to the surface. I had been stuffing and numbing the pain of my biological father abandoning me. Additionally, I was dealing with the pain and confusion caused by my stepfather molesting me as a child. I spent years in therapy, but drinking still had a hold on me.

When I was 48-years-old, after thirty-four years of living with my addiction, I finally went to my first Alcoholic Anonymous (AA) meeting. I started working the AA 12 Step program, each step taking me deeper to the core of my addiction. When I reached Step Eight, forgiveness, I finally uncovered years of unfulfilled expectations, which I had of others and myself. I had not forgiven the father who left or the stepfather who stole my trust. I realized I had not forgiven myself for not being able to measure up and for not being tough enough to handle life.

When I finished Step Eight and Nine, I finally started to live a life free from the guilt and pain, and free from drinking. Forgiving is a freeing process. With the combination of therapy, AA, and my strength in God, I forgave the people who offended me. I forgave myself for being an imperfect human.

Forgiveness is so much more than saying, "I forgive you," hugging it out, and then getting a Frappuccino together. Forgiveness is said to be a path or journey, but a journey makes it sound pleasant and relaxing. In my experience, it is more like a wild rapid ride down a roaring river, getting tossed around, while needing to wear a life jacket. The river takes you on an expedition, gently floating one minute, and thrashing with anger the next. By the end of it you're soaking wet, and your heart is a bit bruised.

At the conclusion of your adventure you will be smarter and wiser. You will be able to stand on the virtual shore, paddle held high above your head in victory! You have forgiven, you have learned, and you have survived. You will be ready to move forward, ultimately experiencing better relationships.

Forgiveness in Major Religions

I love religion. I love the sacred texts, color, ceremony, and music of each and every religion on this planet. Christianity is my home religion (Jesus is my guy!) I know I am rare today, but I have learned many deep lessons from every religion.

People are currently afraid of religion, and for good reason. A lot of people have done very bad things in the name of their religion. Many people profess peace and reconciliation, all the while committing violence in the name of God. This is not a new problem. The religious wars that waged in Europe lasted over 100 years (mid-1500's to mid-1600's) and pitted Catholics against Protestants. Fast forward to the 21st century, and not much has changed. Jews and Palestine Muslims are fighting for land that is 25 miles long and about seven miles wide. Muslim Extremists commit terrorist attacks in the name of Allah all over the world.

When the topic of religion is brought up, many people's immediate reactions are swift and rigid. People fear you are going to try to convert, contort, or convince them of something different than what they are securely and comfortably rooted in. The reason they are securely and comfortably rooted is because of their own personal experience. Where we live, how old we are, our family, and our lifelong experiences form our beliefs.

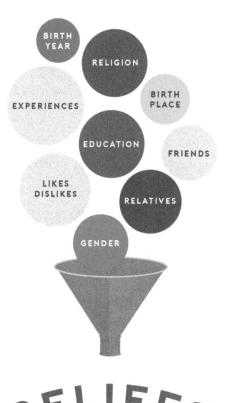

I know western religion brings up visions of stuffed shirts spouting hell and damnation, and many times leaving out Jesus' intent of love and acceptance. All religions have rules that are set down in sacred scripture. Clergy, rabbis, deacons, monks, and nuns are human beings who interpret these rules. Many times, these interpretations are to support our own human agendas.

Don't get me wrong, rules are important. These sacred scriptures are our guidebooks to a healthy and productive life. However, every religion seems to interpret every line item on Heaven, Hell, God, right, wrong, prophet, or saint, differently, leaving us all feeling conflicted, judged, and occasionally scared.

I do not like being preached at any more than the next person. I have never had anyone yell at me for twenty minutes and have me change my mind. This is when religion becomes dogma and loses the intent of the loving spirit of God. A good sermon does not yell at you, a good sermon teaches, informs, and touches your heart. Who wants to go to church, temple, or synagogue, only to add on to the internal shame or the external blame we already deal with? We want to be lovingly guided, forgiven, and accepted.

Some religions conjure up issues of culture clashes that seem angry, foreign, and fanatical. How can we ever be good enough for God when we are not even good enough for each other? We are being told that how we pray, worship, and see God is wrong only because it doesn't look the same way as others pray, worship, and see God. Aren't we missing the point? It can get overwhelming and confusing.

Good news. When it comes to the subject of forgiveness, all the major religions sing a common song. It is better for you to let it go. God is big on forgiveness; human-to-human forgiveness, and the spiritual type. Forgiveness is one of the common threads in all religions. Let's call it the golden thread that ties all the major religions together. Forgiveness rescues us from being flawed human beings, no matter how you worship.

I have given a short breakdown of each major religion and their take on forgiveness. I hope you find it helpful.

Christianity

 Forgiveness is central to Christianity, and Jesus is the fundamental figure of Christianity. Jesus fulfills the prophecy of the Old Testament. He hung on a cross and died to bring forgiveness for the sins of all man.

Jesus was born of a virgin and is the son of God. For some people, even Christians, that is a tough one to wrap your head around. God, Jesus' father, sent Jesus to experience the pain and suffering of man. To experience what we do to ourselves every day, and to help us selfish humans become selfless, with a dose of true forgiveness.

In the last two thousand plus years since Jesus' short thirty-three years of life, I would say humanity has progressed at a snail's pace on Jesus' message of tolerance, acceptance, and the "love thy neighbor" thing.

Jesus hung out with troublemakers, the poor, the sinners. Jesus denounced the righteous religious leaders who were more about personal power than worshiping God. Jesus was not against religion; he went to temple and worshiped. Jesus' message was for everyone, pious to poor, because we are all sinners.

Forgiveness is mentioned thirty-two times in the New Testament, and seventy-four times in the Bible overall. One of the most quoted parables regarding forgiveness in Christianity is Matthew 18:21.

The Parable of the Unmerciful Servant

Peter, Jesus' disciple, came to Jesus and asked, "Jesus, how many times shall I forgive someone who has hurt me?" and Jesus told Peter, "Up to seventy times seven." Seventy times seven equals a lot. This is interpreted as "without number, endless." Then Jesus went on to tell the story about a servant that owed a King ten thousand bags of gold. The King was going to throw his family in jail until he repaid the debt. The servant begged and pleaded with the King to let his family go. The King took mercy on him and his family, canceled the debt, and let the family go. Then that same servant left the castle and bumped right into an old friend who owed him a small bag of silver. Bet you can guess what the servant did. He demanded that he pay him back. The old friend was just as destitute as he was, and could not pay him back. But the servant went screaming to the authorities to have him arrested and thrown in jail. What was Jesus trying to point out? Forgive, as you have been forgiven.

What do you want to say about that parable? I know what I want to say. Cheats and scoundrels have been around for a long time! How easy we forget the kindness given to us by others in our life. It is remarkable how a story more than two thousand years old can still hold its power today.

I want to take a quick pause for the forgiveness cause here. Often, in one-on-one sessions and workshops, I hear faithful Christians say they want to forgive a person who has truly harmed them. They struggle because they feel that Jesus' teaching is saying they must let the person back into their life once they forgive them. I cannot speak for Jesus. I am not a theologian and do not fully understand every scripture. But I have never spoken to a theologian or another clergy who has not agreed with me. The Bible does not say you should let anyone hurt you physically, mentally, spiritually or emotionally. Yes, forgive seventy times seven, but use what you have learned to create healthy boundaries.

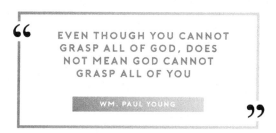

> " EVEN THOUGH YOU CANNOT GRASP ALL OF GOD, DOES NOT MEAN GOD CANNOT GRASP ALL OF YOU
>
> WM. PAUL YOUNG "

Judaism

In Judaism, forgiveness is taken seriously enough to give it a holiday.

The ten days between Rosh Hashanah (Jewish New Year) and Yom Kippur (the Day of Atonement) are called the ten days of repentance. This is a special time every year to focus on making things right with people you have offended. The day of Yom Kippur is for people in the Jewish faith to pray and fast as they seek God's forgiveness for sins against God.

The Day of Atonement

"The tenth of the seventh month shall be the Day of Atonement for you. It is a holy holiday when you must fast and bring a fire offering to God. Do not do any work on this day; it is a day of atonement, when you gain atonement before God your God." (VaYikra 23:27-28).

God does not grant human-to-human forgiveness. If you have hurt someone, it is your responsibility to go to him or her and ask for forgiveness. And not just a quick I am sorry, but sincerely three times. This is teshuvah, or repentance. Once you have repented, and made amends it is the responsibility of the offended person to forgive.

The glaring difference between Judaism and other major religions, such as Christianity is that repentance from the wrong doer is needed to grant forgiveness. Not from God but from the wounded victim. In other religions, forgiveness for sins against others is granted when you ask God to pardon you.

"And at the moment when the sinner asks for forgiveness – forgive with a whole heart and a desirous soul. And even if he pained him and sinned against him many times, he should not take revenge or hold a grudge -- that is the way of the Children of Israel and their correct hearts." (Mishneh Torah 2:10 Repentance)

In Judaism, a murder is unforgiveable because the murderer cannot ask for forgiveness from the murder victim. The murder must answer to God for the crime. The family of the victim can forgive the murder for the grief that the murder caused them. Again, the murder must show repentance and submit to the punishment for the crime.

Hinduism

Hinduism, like many faiths, is diverse and influenced by culture. If you are in India there is not a word for forgiveness, because forgiveness is something expected. But here in the United States our culture teaches forgiveness. Hindu teachers are now introducing teachings on forgiveness.

One Hindu tradition that helps with this view on the topic of forgiveness is a theistic perspective, a teaching on "the one supreme peace" the Bhagavad Gita, which lists forgiveness as a Divine characteristic. (Mahabharata, Udyoga Parva Section XXXIII) And who would not want to be Divine?

We see the law of karma in Hindu. In the west, we use the word karma to justify something bad happening to someone. If a grumpy neighbor has a tree fall on their car, we say, "Oh, karma is a bitch." But is that really karma? Karma in Hinduism is much more than a tree falling on a car. Bad karma is what binds someone's soul (Atman) to birth and rebirth. Karma is reflected in one's class, disposition, and character in life.

Yes, you can work on karma in your current life. Prarabdha Karma is the karma you experience during the present lifetime. Next time you want to say, "Karma's a bitch," just add, "Prarabdha Karma is a bitch." In your lifetime, you create good and bad karma that you carry forward. What you do matters, and the goal is to achieve a release from the cycle of birth and rebirth, learning to create no more karma.

In the reform movements of Hinduism, you will find a concept of Divine grace called Kripa, from Bhakti Yoga. It means, "grace," "mercy," or "blessings," depending on where it is used. Kripa is the central tenet of Bhakti Yoga and Bhakti movements. With Kripa, you can transcend lifetimes of karma.

Krishna (an Indian divinity that is the 8th incarnation of the Hindu God, Vishnu) refers to Kripa, grace, forgiveness, and mercy in the final chapter of the Bhagavad Gita. Verse 18.66, "Setting aside all meritorious deeds (Dharma), just surrender completely to my will (with firm faith and loving contemplation), I shall liberate you from all sins. Do not fear."

Islam

Islam is similar to Christianity and Judaism regarding forgiveness. Allah (God) is merciful and forgiving, understanding that human beings are not perfect.

There are two types of forgiveness in Islam; Allah's and human. "O Allah! Make me among those who, when they commit an act of virtue, feel good, and when they commit a mistake, they seek forgiveness." (Ibn Majah) Allah forgives and forgets when his servants ask for forgiveness honestly. "It is He who accepts repentance from His servants and pardons bad deeds and knows whatever you do." (Ash-Shura 42:25) "And those who avoid the major sin and immoralities, and when they are angry, they forgive" (Surat ash-Shu'ara 42:37) In both instances of forgiveness, from Allah or from others it is important to rectify the mistake.

Islam has ninety-nine names for God, "Al-Ghaffar – the most forgiving one" – is one of them.

In Islam, as opposed to Judaism, you do not need the offender to apologize or ask for forgiveness. Forgiveness is about you and for you. Of course, if someone has done you wrong, a good heartfelt apology is helpful in reconciliation. If there is repentance, it will bring a better bond between the two offending parties. However, forgiveness does not require repentance by the offender.

If you want to be forgiven you must forgive others, especially if you seek forgiveness from God. When you seek forgiveness, you humble yourself. When you give your forgiveness, you show your true generosity. Choosing forgiveness brings happiness by improving our earthly relationships and the reward of Allah's forgiveness for our own human lacking.

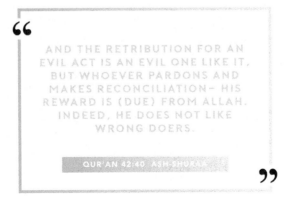

"
AND THE RETRIBUTION FOR AN EVIL ACT IS AN EVIL ONE LIKE IT, BUT WHOEVER PARDONS AND MAKES RECONCILIATION— HIS REWARD IS (DUE) FROM ALLAH. INDEED, HE DOES NOT LIKE WRONG DOERS.

QUR'AN 42:40 ASH-SHURAA
"

Modern Spirituality

Today's Modern Spirituality, also called New Age, has become more focused on the good parts of the various different religions, leaving the more controlling parts behind. I know many people in traditional religions look at modern spirituality as a bit of God and "magical woo, woo" with a dash of hippie love put in one cosmic blender turned up on high. I get it. Coming from a lifelong, very traditional religious background, modern spirituality does look like you are always at a party. However, know that modern seekers of the Divine tend to see all religions as one. Even though God is known by different names according to the specific religion, we all emerge from the same place, and share the commonality that all are connected to one God.

Forgiveness carries over to the New Age tradition as well. Forgiveness is said to alleviate your energetic (and physical body) of pent-up resentment and suffering. If this pent-up suffering is left to fester, it could lead to many types of disease.

Forgiveness in modern spirituality usually involves meditations and prayers. In the meditations and prayers, you send love and light to the person or situation to be forgiven. There is also the idea that the biggest part of our forgiveness usually lies in forgiving ourselves. Forgiving the judgment we put on ourselves for our own mistakes and misdeeds.

The Faith to Forgive

Faith is to have belief without proof. This is a very hard concept for anyone. Faith is intertwined in our experiences, hopes, and dreams. Faith tells us that even though we do not understand why things happen, we will be OK. That if we are sad, we will be happy again. If we feel empty, we will be loved again. Faith considers that something better is just around the corner. Forgiveness needs faith; faith that you will have a brighter tomorrow. Faith that your tomorrow will be without the anger and pain you feel today.

On your forgiveness journey, you need to believe in your strength to forgive the situation, the person, or even yourself. Faith gives you hope that your life will be happy, secure, and free from the control of your sad and negative emotions. When you are forgiving, faith helps you move past the pain and gives hope for the future.

How do we have this faith? Some people seem to be born with more faith than others, the ultimate "glass half full" person. But, most of us gain our faith from the wisdom of life experience. When you have gone through a bad situation and survived, maybe even thrived in spite of difficult circumstances, your faith grows.

Faith in God comes when you make the decision to believe. When you are a child, you have faith in what you are told to believe in, or not believe in. As you grow, you have to choose to have faith in God. With maturity, you have the discernment to decide if you believe in God. Your faith in God also comes from surviving difficult circumstances and seeing God's hand in your life.

In the Bible, faith can be described as "small as a mustard seed." I am glad this is all I need because at times in my life I have doubted deeply. Have you? Doubt is normal. God does not want your blind faith. God wants you to believe because you see and feel your faith. Love is something we believe in because we have felt it. Faith is also something you feel.

Take comfort in knowing that doubting that there is a God is perfectly human, regardless of spirituality. Next time you are at the grocery store, buy some mustard seeds and put a few in your wallet. They are very small. It will remind you that faith as small as a mustard seed is powerful.

YOUR THOUGHTS:

UNDERSTANDING FORGIVENESS

CHAPTER FOUR

We only need to forgive because we pick up un-forgiveness. What is un-forgiveness? It is that ugly feeling that can either show up in the blink of an eye, or via smoldering resentment that builds up over time. These are feelings that usually come from unfulfilled expectations. Are these un-forgiveness feelings idealistic? In most cases, they are not. Most people have typical expectations of other people, situations, and ourselves.

When a person or situation hits us with a hard blow of emotional pain, it hurts and we feel it. It is a punch in the gut, heart, head, and soul. Often the anger is temporary, but the hurt remains. What you choose to do with that anger and pain after the initial blow is your decision. This is your defining moment. This is where it becomes all about you. This is where you get to take back your power and triumph over the abuser. Working through the pain and anger is what makes you strong. Forgiveness is about your strength, not the other person's weaknesses.

Situational un-forgiveness occurs when an event transpires in our life that was not part of the plan. There are many examples of situational un-forgiveness; losing a job, illness strikes, or a natural disaster hits. Situational forgiveness is something that changes our everyday life into a crisis.

Who do you blame when tragedy overtakes your life? Some people blame God. "If God is so powerful, then why did God not stop this terrible thing?" Some people blame others around them, our society, or even themselves. We are all surprised when a lightning bolt hits our life out of a clear blue sky. That is when we can pick up situational un-forgiveness. **Here are just a few reasons I have heard for picking up un-forgiveness:**

Your turn...Fill in the blank with your un-forgiveness.

Forgiveness...What It Is and What It Is Not

Are we supposed to forgive and forget? Is forgiving unconditional? How do we forgive a perfect stranger? Even harder, how do we forgive someone we have loved and trusted, when that love and trust is broken? To answer these questions, it is important to understand what forgiveness is, and what it is not.

Forgiveness does not fix the problems; it recognizes the problems. You can be right and forgive. You can be wrong and forgive. You can be neither right nor wrong and still forgive.

During the beginning of my workshops and talks, I start by asking the audience what they believe forgiveness to be, based on their experience of it. During one workshop, I noticed a middle-aged woman sitting with her hands clasped tightly together, looking a bit nervous. Her nervous hand shot up at my question, and she gave me her definition of what forgiveness is. "Forgiving is required by God, and you must give the person another chance to be in your life." I hear this often. This is the old "forgive and forget" rule written by someone, and then hammered into a stone tablet, dictating that you must give everyone a second, third or 100th chance.

The rest of her family was putting undeniable pressure on her to forgive and forget, as a Christian should do. She also felt a force she perceived, coming down from the heavens to add an extra layer of spiritual pressure. The reason she was struggling was simple. She loved the family member that needed forgiveness, but she did not trust him. This is a perfect example of someone who is being told that love should conquer everything unconditionally.

I don't know when our society and all the major religions twisted forgiveness into a knot of unhealthy boundaries and confusing requests. There is a misunderstanding in our current culture's mentality that says if you forgive, you are condoning the actions of the offender, and you must forget it ever happened. I have never met a person who was cheated on, lied to, or whose child was murdered, who forgot the event ever occurred, even when they were able to forgive the offense. Humans and elephants have long memories. Why? So, we stay safe. Whether you are staring down a snake in the grass, or you're at a family reunion, God gave us that special mechanism so we would walk away from danger, not keep running back to it. We need to learn from the things that happen to us, and the stupid things we do. We are supposed to learn so we don't repeat them. That way we can live healthy, happy lives.

Oftentimes trust is confused with forgiveness. Forgiveness is not trust. Trust is earned, and it can take time. You can forgive someone for their bad behavior but you do not have to trust that they will not do it again. Whatever "it" is. They are on their path and their journey. Forgiveness does not require that you trust a person or a situation. Stay out of their path!

In Christianity, you often hear the term, "Separating the sin from the sinner." This is an expression used to help you, the forgiver, see the action as evil or wrong, but not the person. Now before you start wiggling in your seat, getting ready to tell me that there are vile people out there, and separating what they did from who they are is impossible. I might agree with you. But ask yourself, are you their judge, jury, and jailer? Do you have the authority to sentence them for the crime? You can say what they did was wrong, immoral, or hurtful, and I'm sure you are right. However, it doesn't matter that you're right in the case of forgiveness. You can leave the judging of their soul to God, and the judging of their flesh to the judicial system, and in the case of harmful people, you can decide upon setting healthy boundaries.

Letting forgiveness happen is like taking a step back from the situation, taking a deep breath, and allowing the pain to leave as you exhale. Forgiveness does not mean you forget what happened. Forgiveness does not mean the person who offended you is not accountable for their actions. What it does mean is that you are no longer their jailer in the "cells" of your heart and mind. You can now stop trying to change what already happened. Newsflash: They had no idea you locked them up in the prison. Really, you have been the one jailed by the pain and suffering. It is time to open the gate and let the pain out.

Recently, I was working with a young woman who was distressed about her sister, who has been addicted to several different drugs for years. She loves her sister, which makes it even harder. The sister had been in the cycle of rehab and relapse many times. The woman took her sister into her home only to have her steal her precious possessions to pawn to get money for drugs. She was tired of the situation, and she was angry. Her exact words were, "I can't forgive my sister. If I forgive her, it'll only happen all over again." When I offered her a genuine solution that would allow her to forgive her sister, go on loving her sister, but keep healthy boundaries, she let out a big sigh of relief. She said, "You mean I can forgive my sister and still not have a relationship with her?" Yes, you can!

It is amazing how love can still exist in places where anger and sadness have lived for so long. It is hard when we see how great people could be, yet they do not see it in themselves. You just want to sit them down, grab them, shake them, and yell, "WAKE UP! You're wasting your life and I love you! Please get better, be healthy, and live a good life." However, that doesn't work. We make decisions because of our pain and some people, like this young woman's sister, are struggling more than others. You can still love them, pray for them, and help them within healthy boundaries. This keeps you in a good place. Love them from afar.

If you thumb through a dictionary or type in "forgiveness" on your computer, you will find that forgiveness is a verb. It is a thing you do. "Forgiveness is the act of forgiving something or someone." To forgive, according to Webster's online dictionary is, "To give up resentment of, or claim to, requital for, to cease to feel resentment against (an offender)." It's hard to stop feeling resentment. We are not programmed to give up, or to stop bad feelings on a whim. If we give up, then what does that mean? They win, we lose? Is the word 'wimp,' also under the definition of 'forgiveness?' It sounds like it. However, I promise, it is not. Rather, forgiveness is for the strong-minded and strong-willed.

Forgiveness is a choice you make. You have the power here. I don't know you personally. I don't know what and whom you are struggling to forgive. However, I do know that when we've been hurt physically, mentally, and/or emotionally, we can lose our personal power. Forgiveness lets us take that back.

Many people do not have a chance to face the offenders who have severely hurt them. The loss of personal power can be huge. To be able to use the authority of forgiveness in oneself can help renew what was once so cruelly taken away. In a later exercise, we'll see how to use this authority to take back what was taken, by virtually having your "Day in Court." This is a chance to tell your offender how they hurt you.

Many times, we decide to tell someone we forgive him or her, not because we really have, but because we want him or her to say they are sorry. We want them to admit they are wrong even if it was just a little bit. This helps feed our need to be right and calms our inner brain.

Before my brother Glenn died, I had planned on telling him that I had forgiven him for his past actions and behavior. The problem with this very righteous plan of mine was that he might not have felt he had done anything worthy of needing forgiveness. Or even if he agreed that his behavior was wrong, he may not have been very receptive to me pointing it out.

Now, if I had taken my case to a judge, I could have proven he had done many things to hurt me, my family, and even himself. I could paint a grim picture of him and make sure he looked like the bad guy at all times. What I was missing, even as a trained reverend, was that I had not forgiven him at all. I was still holding out for him to agree with me – agree that he was the villain in my life. I still wanted an "I am sorry," and to prove I was right. It does not matter whether I was right. I was not his judge and jury. Life is about free will. He could live his life as he chose to live it, even if those choices hurt others.

Was it okay for me to tell my brother that his actions hurt me? Yes! You are welcome to have a conversation with anyone. You can tell people that their actions are not okay with you. But before you do, you will need to decide if that conversation would help the situation. Many times, people do not want to hear their wrongs listed to them like they are five years old. Even if you hand them a list of their crimes against you, it does not mean they will admit to them. Tread lightly here. Do not lecture, but speak from your heart. It will have a more powerful impact.

You have the right to protect yourself from harm. If you were born in the twentieth century or watched any TV program post-Brady Bunch, you know the term "healthy boundaries." (More on this subject in Chapter 8). It is okay to tell somebody his or her actions hurt you and what your boundaries are. The person may still not agree, even if you have kindly stated your boundaries and limits. You are informing, not looking for agreement.

If someone asks you for forgiveness, you do not have to give it to him or her, just as they do not have to forgive you. If they are acknowledging the wrong they have done to you, and are trying to make amends or apologize, (who doesn't love a good apology?) it's your decision to accept that apology or not.

There is no secret window into your soul or anyone else... nope not even through the eyes. If you decide to forgive someone they will never know if you truly do because, as I have mentioned before, forgiveness happens in your heart, mind, and soul only. It is true that people cannot see into your soul. What people do see are your actions. If you have truly forgiven, usually your actions change. You do not walk around speaking negative things about the person. Nor do you sit around waiting for an apology.

Below I have listed what forgiveness is, and what forgiveness is not, in my words. I recommend that you write down what forgiveness is to you, and what forgiveness is not to you, in your own words.

FORGIVENESS...

...IS YOUR CHOICE	...IS NOT FORGETTING
...IS A DECISION TO STOP TRYING TO CONTROL A PERSON OR A SITUATION	...IS NOT SAYING WHAT HAPPENED WAS OKAY
...IS TAKING RESPONSIBILITY FOR YOUR ACTIONS AND MAKING AMENDS	...IS NOT LETTING THE PERSON OUT OF JUSTICE
...IS A LONELY BUSINESS (HAPPENS IN YOUR SOUL, HEART, + MIND ONLY)	...IS NOT LETTING THE PERSON OUT OF THE CONSEQUENCES
...IS HAVING HEALTHY BOUNDARIES	...IS NOT SAYING YOU WILL NO LONGER BE SAD OR WISH IT WERE DIFFERENT

Forgiveness Can Be A Lonely Business

I think you understand my point. Forgiveness is deeply personal. It's about healing from the pain others have caused you, or the pain you've caused yourself. It is about deciding to give yourself the gift of learning from the experience. You are learning to recognize danger coming your way. You are recognizing that you are starting to do something that later you will regret. You are also learning that you are in charge of your emotions and your reaction to others' behavior. Everyone makes mistakes, including you.

41

True forgiveness is not superficial. Forgiveness is deep and soul changing. But it does take practice. It is much easier to forgive somebody who cut you off in traffic than it is to forgive someone who has betrayed your trust or hurt you physically, emotionally, or spiritually. The practice of forgiving the small stuff on a daily basis will help you when you have to tackle the big stuff.

Situational Forgiveness

Situational forgiveness is forgiving what happened so you can stop being angry. Situational forgiveness can be hard because it is unlike forgiving a person, you cannot have empathy for cancer or natural disasters.

Situational forgiveness can teach us some of our greatest lessons. Have you ever met someone who has come through cancer treatment and said that it changed their lives? And it changed their lives for the better. Many times, an unexplained situation, even the really bad ones, can catapult us to a better life. Tough situations can bring out strength we never knew we had.

Here is my story of situational forgiveness.

My Broken Back – The Crack Heard Around the World! A Story of Situational Forgiveness

On November 15, 2008, a sudden and unexpected event happened. I was in the gym with a professional trainer, trying to turn my 42-year old body back into the 25-year old version of myself. I wanted to achieve chiseled arms, and lift my butt a few precious inches. The idea of gaining physical strength was an added bonus. However, as I sweat and exercised, little did I know that this was the last day I would feel strong again for many years.

At the end of my hour-long training session, I was ready to end big. I stood in front of the weight bar with 50 plus pounds on each side, toes perfectly positioned under the bar, body straight, ready to lower myself down into a squat position to pick up the bar and weights. I grabbed the bar, started to straighten, using all my thighs and lower back muscles to get the weight to up above my knees. Suddenly I felt like I had been hit from behind with a baseball bat. I am not sure if my trainer heard the intense scream first or whether he saw my body start to crumble. I put the weight back on the floor. Or maybe I dropped it. How does one remember

42

when they have just been with hit an electrified baseball bat?

I thought I had pulled one of my new extra strong muscles. My trainer sent me home with strict instructions to put ice on my muscles, rest, and relax. But I had different plans. I was taking the first girly trip away since my sixth and last child was born. I had a long, kid-free drive and two kid-free days planned in Las Vegas with friends. Sure, my pulled muscle hurt but I was sure that painkillers and a heated car seat would relax the pain away.

I pulled into the large hotel with dreams of a spa day and dinner out, dressed in my best high heels. Like a real woman, not the yoga pants and scruffy t-shirt mom that was my everyday reality. I pulled up to the valet, opened my door, and found myself stuck. My legs would not turn to get out of the car. The pain was overwhelming. I thought the painkillers must have worn off. The dapper looking valet helped me get out of the car and I hobbled into the lobby. Soon I was in my room. I took more painkillers and a long soak in a warm bath and started getting ready to meet the girls and hit the town.

A few hours later, I knew I was in trouble. After months of workouts my toned, strengthened body felt more like a bag of unconnected bones. I took more painkillers and did not move from the bed. The next day, over-whelmed with pain, I realized I had to get home and go to a doctor.

When I went to see my family doctor the next day, I was put on narcotic pain medication and a dose of steroids. Still thinking I had pulled a mus-cle, I hoped for a quick full recovery. I was convinced that I had pulled a muscle. I had gone through childbirth, so I thought I could handle a pulled muscle. Until I knew I couldn't.

A few days after my first doctor's visit, I could barely function. My next appointments were for an MRI scan and an orthopedic back doctor. I still thought I'd be able to get my back fixed with time and medication. As I perched on the exam table of the orthopedic doctor, trying not to look like the biggest wimp on the planet, sweat rolled down my face from the excruciating pain shooting from my lower back into my legs. My body was not holding things together.

A handsome, white-coated surgeon walked into the little exam room. In all my years working with doctors, handsome was a word I rarely used when describing physicians. Usually, doctors looked like the science nerds in high school that revealed the truth in the saying, "You have beauty or brains." This well-respected, tanned, orthopedic surgeon with amazing hair had both. What are the odds? He politely shook my hand and said, "Nice to meet you. I've seen your scans. And I don't usually get to say this when I first meet a patient, but your back is broken and you need surgery." I was so surprised I thought I would fall off the exam table and chance a broken leg.

This is a moment I have come to call, "Having your ticket punched." I was about to take a trip I had not planned on, a trip that would take me into dark times filled with physical and emotional pain. We all come up against these unpredicted moments in our life from time to time, interrupting our regular day and our regular problems. My ticket had just been punched, and for me it was a broken back. For others, it could be a cancer diagnosis, an MS diagnosis, a car accident, or the death of a loved one that sets you out on a journey you had not planned for.

Broken back! What and how? The doctor explained that I had something called Spondylolisthesis (a condition where the vertebra moves forward) and two Pars Interarticularis (butterfly looking bones on each side of your vertebra), fractures in my L5 vertebra. In simple terms, my spine had moved forward and both bones on each side of the vertebra had broken in half. Those butterfly wing bones were just floating there, hitting some major nerves and causing major pain. So now I knew it was not a pulled muscle.

Surgery was something I did not want. In all my years in the medical field, I had seen back patients have multiple surgeries, and still they ended up with decreased movement and continuing pain. A vision of the electric grocery store scooters shot through my mind. Heck, no! I was not going to end up that way. So, I declined surgery. The handsome doctor was also kind, and he said, "It's okay, I'll be here when you need me. In the meantime, here's a referral for a pain doctor and a prescription for stronger narcotic pain medication."

Throughout the next nine months, I had twelve injections in my back and two types of physical therapy. I was now taking up to ten narcotic pain pills a day to try to function. But I was not functioning. I was mad this happened to me. I was mad at God. I was mad at my body for giving out. I had eaten right, I exercised, and I was still young according to society's standards. This back injury was not a part of my life plan. I had many reasons for situational un-forgiveness.

I thought I was working hard to get better, until I found myself in line at the pharmacy to get yet another bottle of pain medication. The line at the pharmacy was long. *Standing for any period of time was excruciating. All I could think about was my back. I am not sure how the person behind me struck up a friendly conversation, but they did. The person did not ask, but I told them my full back story (pun intended). Details and pain you would only share with a good friend, not a stranger in line to get their blood pressure medicine. I revealed my physical pain, the use of pain pills, and how unfair this back injury was. Finally, the moving line made me stop telling my sad story. It was my turn to pick up my large bottle of pain medication.*

As I walked away from the pharmacy counter, I saw the woman shoot me a look of pity. I am sure she felt bad for me, but at the same time, I am sure she did not want to be my new best friend. When I got to my car, I cried. I had turned into a victim. I was a victim of this very unfair situation. I was mad and sad. This situation had turned me into that person you never want to run into at a party or a pharmacy. We have all been stuck with a person who cannot talk about anything else but the injustice and pain of whatever has happened to them. It is not that you or most people do not care, but no one wants to be friends with a condition, or the victim of the condition.

If you ever find yourself in this position, ask yourself if your story is confirming your pain and cementing your identity as a victim. Mine was, and I needed to do something to change the story line.

I went back to the kind handsome doctor and told him I knew it was time to have the surgery. I wish I could have said this calmly, but I burst into tears and told the surgeon, "I can't take the pain anymore." I was referring to both the physical and mental pain.

My back-fusion surgery took seven hours. Nuts, bolts, and a cage went around my spine to hold it all together like a finished jigsaw puzzle. I woke up in recovery, feeling groggy as expected. Almost instantly I realized that the pain was gone. I had surgical pain, and that was painful, but the disconnected nerve and bone pain I had lived with for nine months was finally gone. I broke down and I started to cry. Relief flooded through me, the fear of surgery was gone, and hope had been restored.

Recovery was hard. I was in a walker. I could not even get on or off the toilet on my own. I was fitted with a large back brace that had a pulley system so I could tighten it like a corset. My husband and dear friends took turns being my care provider. My youngest son was three years old, and I could not do any more than kiss his cheeks when he visited me on my bed.

I wore a device called a bone stimulator. It had electrodes that stuck to my skin around my lower back and sent low level pulses. The goal was to encourage my bones to grow together. I was an outstanding recovery patient. I put all my determination into becoming better. Within three months, I was walking without my walker, wearing only the giant back brace and the electrodes.

Over the next seven months, I had done so many x-rays I lost count. I also had an MRI to confirm my bones were knitting back together. Then one afternoon, soon after an MRI scan, my cell phone rang. It was my surgeon. He had a sympathetic tone as he let me know my back was not knitting itself together. I would need another fusion, this time adding cadaver bone to hopefully get my bones to grow together. My ears heard his words, but my legs gave way. Kneeling on the floor, I listened to him tell me I had to go through it all over again. When was God going to reward me for my hard work? I felt a familiar anger and sadness overtake me.

My old un-forgiveness had been renewed. My second surgery was even longer than my first. Fortunately, recovery did move faster. I was a pro with a walker, a pulley back brace, and a bone stimulator. Four months after my second surgery, the new MRI showed evidence of bone growth. My heart sent a prayer of thanks to the person who died and donated their bone.

As my bone increased, my narcotic use decreased. There were moments where I did not think about my back. Chronic pain, even when it's at a low level, is exhausting. A smart pain doctor once described chronic pain to my husband as, "It's like putting your hand on your stove burner, set to low. Keep your hand there 24 hours a day, seven days a week. Now try to have a normal day."

During my recovery from my second surgery, a friend of mine sat at the end of my bed and told me I needed to do a triathlon. I laughed through my narcotic haze. A triathlon? I could barely walk, and even the old me hated running.

My friend had fought her own battles. Her ticket had been punched years before with a diagnosis of Multiple Sclerosis and ten lesions on her brain. She was a young mom of four at the time of her diagnosis. She had clawed her way back to health through swimming, biking, and running. A year later, I decided to take the challenge.

It is true that we need mentors. We need to know that others have succeeded. My friend cheered me on as I started my training. My training started out with walking, slow swims, and a new bike. Slowly, I increased *my strength. And on a spring San Diego day, with my friends and family cheering me on, I crossed the finish line, vomited, and joyfully finished my first triathlon.*

Since that first triathlon I have completed six more. I did something I could not, or would not have even tried before I broke my back. My reasons for working out had gone from trying for chiseled arms and a higher butt, to being able to walk.

I had another six-hour surgery to remove the nuts and bolts that once held me together. I still struggle with chronic pain. I know that staying physically strong is the only way to stay out of electronic scooter shopping carts for years to come.

I do not know why my bones broke that day. My forgiveness of the situation had to happen to release the anger I had towards the years of pain and the disappointment in my own body for breaking. I had to look back at the years and find the lessons. I needed to change my perspective. What I found was lessons about my own stubbornness, and deep gratitude for everyone who showed up for me.

I am thankful for my friends and family who took care of me at my darkest moments. I am thankful for the brilliantly skilled surgeons who stood for hours in surgery to repair my broken bones. I am thankful for the mental and physical strength I never knew I had. I have been able to forgive the situation that punched my ticket and put me on that long unexpected journey.

WORK IT QUESTIONS

Look at the chart, What Forgiveness Is and Is Not.

What would you add?

Did you have some misconceptions about forgiveness? If so, what were they?

Have you known someone that was faced with a tough situation and you were inspired by their strength? If so, who and why? (You can pick yourself)

CONSTRUCT
CHAPTER FIVE

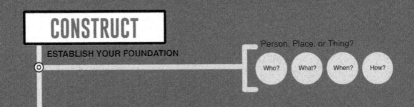

STEP 1 - Construct
Construct your story and establish your foundation.

Sitting on the First Step of Forgiveness

One day a client who was struggling to forgive her father said, "I want to forgive but I can't get past the, 'I want.'" How perfect is that? Often, we desperately want to let stuff go and move on. But our minds and emotions are holding on to everything. They're on a hamster wheel turning over and over in our heads, trying to change what has already happened. Just like my client, she wanted to be move past the pain. She wanted to forgive. However, her mind was still stuck replaying all that happened while her heart was trying to change the past.

It is very hard when the person you acknowledged you want to forgive, keeps giving you reasons for more un-forgiveness. Most people do not just commit one offense, especially in long term relationships. People rack up offenses one on top of the other. After you have gone through the Forgiveness Algorithm, you will have the skills to forgive, and forgive again.

All journeys start at the beginning, but getting to the beginning can be tough. We all know that people who choose to never forgive can lead a bitter and angry life. Every decision they make stems from the pain they carry. What happened to them could be very worthy of piles anger and pain. But is it worth giving up a whole life for? If it is, then the person or situation that caused the pain wins.

Forgiveness is an inner expedition for an outer offense. Depending on the offense, it could be a short trip, or you could be on a wild ride that lasts much longer. If someone cuts me off in traffic, I let that go by the time I arrive at the supermarket. However, if someone hurt my children, that could be a lifelong forgiveness ride.

Simply getting to the first step and saying, "I want to forgive, I want to let this go" is a major declaration. Imagine yourself putting your feet on a path, go ahead and wiggle your toes and start stretching. Now imagine yourself looking towards the end of the path. Yes, the path is bumpy and full of potholes. But see the end. It is calm, safe, and just what you need. Right now, you have stepped onto the path by saying, "I want to forgive." Before that, you did not even know the path existed. You only knew what you already had; all those unfilled wishes causing you pain and sadness. How long it takes you to get to the end of your path and how many twists and turns there are, is up to you.

Now that you have more understanding about what forgiveness is and is not, you will be able to take the next step. It is time for you to do the work to get to the ultimate celebrated end. That next step is to look very closely at what happened.

But if you are saying, "What if I can't do it?" that is totally normal. It is hard to change and it is hard to let go of pain that is so familiar. With the Forgiveness Algorithm, you have the next steps mapped out for you. It is still your unique journey. What I did is make a map for your route. You are the one that will make the pit stops. On the pit stops you will be putting in the effort so you can mend.

Sure, you are only on the first step, but you have started your journey. Many people do not choose to try. They would rather stay victims of what someone or something did to them, ultimately making the sad or terrible event define them and their life. That is not who you are. You have decided to do something about the resentment and hurt.

Forgiveness is both emotional and decisional. Making a decision to try to forgive will help you with the emotional letting go. Putting a person or situation on a list to forgive is the beginning. It is the first decision on your journey.

Who Do You Want to Forgive?

Who or what do you want to forgive? If you have a complicated situation, your story could involve many people. You will need to work on each person individually. If you picked up this book with the intention of forgiving only one person, then I want you to expand your list. I know you have other people and situations to forgive, because you are human. Start with your top three for now.

I will show you my list to give you an example. My list contains people and a tough situation.

1. Twin brother   2. Mother   3. Broken back

Your list

1.

2.

3.

How To Write Your Story

Let's get started.

Look at your list carefully. How are these people or situations connected? Is the connection only you? Do they affect your life today, or is this an old resentment? This is important for you to clearly figure out the "what" that you want to work through the Forgiveness Algorithm.

Who should you work on forgiving first? It might not be who you originally started with. Yes, your ex-spouse causes you more issues now, and you are dealing with some current anger about them. But, if you have a father who left when you were a child, how long has that hurt been deep inside you? Do you think the old resentment might have affected you now? If you need to shuffle the order of importance, now is the time.

You will gain insight about yourself when you work on un-forgiveness that has affected your life choices. Whoever you choose to work with first, you will find that the process is quicker with others on your list.

Write Yourself Honest

So, why write it down? I know you know your story well. You have told your closest friend, your spouse, and probably even your dog why you are hurt and angry. If this is an old bitterness, you have shaped a story in your head that you have recited for many years. When the story is bouncing between our head and heart, we tend to add or delete important information. Why? Because we need to keep feeding our pain. We need to prove that our story supports our pain. If you heal that pain, the story has no more power.

When I would think about my brother, or tell other people about him, I continuously told the stories about how he hurt my family or me. I would add a dash of how he still did not live a healthy life, to add extra splash. All of this fed my pain and sustained the anger I had towards him.

I would never fill out his part of the story. I would certainly not mention the pain and abuse he suffered and witnessed. If I had, it would have added a layer of compassion. I did not want that. I also never added any fragment of positive things he was or did. I wanted him to be the evilest person living. If he was so evil, then my rude, cold, and angry actions were justified.

Writing the story can change the course of your pain, you can literally write yourself honest. That is what happened when I wrote my story. I wrote the terrible things that had happened to me because they were true. But, when I explained my brother in my story, I had to fill him out. He was not just a one-dimensional villain. That is when his pain jumped off the page. That is when I realized I had written the truth. I wrote myself honest. I could see it completely, like a jigsaw puzzle all put together.

I want you to "write yourself honest." The person you are trying to forgive; a real person. Not just a flat one dimension. Writing and organizing the ins and outs of all that happened can help you uncover some new true reality. You are not giving a person an excuse for their behavior. Just like my brother, he chose to do what he had done. But adding a full picture of him helped me see that he did not have the skills he needed to make different choices.

I understand that words are not always big enough for everything you feel and want to say. I am sorry for that. Therefore, we tend to keep re-running the stories repeatedly in our minds. We try to twist and change the events, desperately searching for the words that would accurately express our pain. Even when you are struggling, words can help you feel less burdened. So, write your story. Use big words, use small tender words, make the words weep with you.

Write Your Story

Look at the three people or situations you want to work on forgiving. Pick one to work on now. Let's follow an outline. Let's pretend your life has become a play, with a cast of characters where you are the lead actor. You have always been the lead actor of your life. God planned it that way.

In a play, you need a plot with twist and turns, ending with the moral of the story. In life, the good guy and bad guy characters can get a bit confused, as often we play both roles. We weigh what is good and what is bad on the scales of justice in our minds. These scales tip one way or the other depending on the person's actions.

Every person has a different set of justice scales in their head to weigh people and their conduct. Some people's scales are not as sensitive as others. That is why you might think someone's behavior is despicable, while someone else might pass it off as mildly irritating. Each person weighs actions based on their individual belief systems, experiences, education, and culture. No two scales will be alike. When you are writing your story, you get to use your scale of justice, and you decide how despicable the behavior is.

WORK IT QUESTIONS

Make sure you are in a comfortable place to write; without distractions, and you have enough time to complete your story. Let's take a moment to breathe. Close your eyes, take a deep breath in, relax, and breathe out.

List the cast of characters in your forgiveness story. Give a brief description of the characters and who they are to you.

Describe the time and place(s) of your story. Set the scene. Describe the when and where it occurred. In the case of long-standing un-forgiveness describe a background with parents/sibling/spouse. What's important is that the story is not too long. One or two pages are enough.

If what happened to you was during your childhood, please take a moment to see yourself as a young you. What was that young you feeling? Write that down. Now, as an adult, how has what happened to you made you different than others? This could be something positive or negative.

Explain where you are now with the person or situation. Do you want the relationship to change? Do you want reconciliation? Maybe you are okay with the current relationship status, but you just want to be able to let go of the bad feelings you have regarding what happened. Write that down.

I have provided pages in this book for you to write out your story. If you need more, use extra paper. You will refer to your story as you work the rest of the Forgiveness Algorithm.

YOUR THOUGHTS:

YOUR THOUGHTS:

EXAMINE
CHAPTER SIX

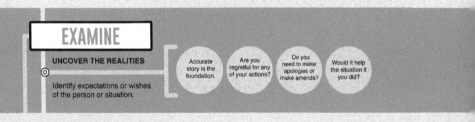

EXAMINE

UNCOVER THE REALITIES

Identify expectations or wishes of the person or situation.

| Accurate story is the foundation. | Are you regretful for any of your actions? | Do you need to make apologies or make amends? | Would it help the situation if you did? |

STEP 2 - Examine
Let's Uncover Your Realities

You wrote down the story of what happened. I know it has been rolling around in your head, heart, and soul for a while. Now the story is out, in black and white, for you to do something with. You might have already discovered a few golden nuggets of wisdom about the situation.

Before you move on to examining your story, I want to share some information that will help you when taking a closer look at your situation. At the end of the chapter you will use your written story to work the questions.

Expectations vs. Reality

I have already mentioned expectations a few times. Let's look at how our expectations affect our reality. Expectations are about anticipation. The hope that someone or some situation will go the way you want it to. When we are knee deep in expectations we can set ourselves up for feelings of un-forgiveness.

Have you ever noticed that when you are upset with someone, often they are surprised you got offended in the first place? People do not understand why you cannot see the situation the same way they do. And you do not understand why they just don't get 'it.' This is because you have different expectations. This is simply because we all come from different backgrounds and beliefs.

When it comes to forgiving someone or situations, it is important that you examine the expectations you have. Every experience you have in your life shapes your future expectations. If you have had bad experiences with a type of person or situation, you will expect that your next encounter will be the same. It will take a positive experience to change your negative expectation. The same is true when you have positive expectations and then have a negative experience.

Wishes, dreams, and expectations are the joys and pitfalls of life. Let's face it, we live on Fantasy Island most of the time. Our minds constantly run all the possibilities that could or should happen. Expecting things to be just how we imagined them. When they do not happen the way we imagined them, we are left with unfulfilled expectations. We are left with ugly feelings of un-forgiveness.

If we had zero expectations of everyone and everything, we would never have any reason to feel let down or mistreated. When your mother, brother, sister, uncle, cousin, friend, husband, wife, or boss do not do what you expected them to do (or be), you get hurt. This is normal. We toss our expectations around all day long, every day of our life. Some are realized, and others are not ever fulfilled.

Various people tend to expect the best and others seem to always expect the worst. I am not sure if it is their DNA or if it is from their upbringing. It's the glass half full or half empty theory. Some of us live in a happy fantasy world with babies and puppies. In turn, other people live in the doom and gloom world of bad witches and flying monkeys all out to get them. Both outlooks are flawed. Life is not always sunny, nor is it always raining. Balancing your expectations will take you out of fantasy land and into a healthy reality.

SOME PEOPLE DO NOT HAVE THE WILL OR THE SKILL TO MEET YOUR EXPECTATIONS.

Will and Skill

When people do not meet our expectations, it is because they do not have the will or the skill. What do I mean by that? Just like it sounds. Even if you have clearly stated to the person your expectation of them or the situation, they might not want to do it. They do not have the will. Other times, we expect from people what they cannot do. They do not have the skill to do what we expect from them. This could be due to mental health issues, addiction, or lack of training. Other times it is a combination of both. People start out with the will, but because of their lack of skill, they lose their will.

This can be so confusing. Many times, at the beginning of relationships; personal or business, everyone thinks you are on the same page. Therefore, contracts are important in business. Clear communication of expectations is also important in our personal lives.

Often, we have expectations of a person and they have no idea what these expectations are. Expectations are sneaky that way. We do not tell our friends, family members, and/or strangers what we expect from them. We expect people to do what we would do or what we think they should do, and we don't even tell them. Then we get offended and expect they should have known. Saying, "They never show up when I need them," "They're always late," "They never help," "That person should have..."

...and so on. If they do not know that you have this expectation of them, the only person who feels upset and let down is you. Whether it is at work, home, church, or school you should always clearly express what you expect from other people.

Adjusting Expectations

Of course, it's not a good idea to walk up to a friend and say, "I expect you to call me three times a week, and if I get sick I expect you to bring cookies." That would sound rather silly. Part of expectations is mirroring. Remember, we teach people how to treat us, and we should mirror how we want to be treated. Then, if the person is not doing or being what you want, you need to ask yourself, "Do they have the will or the skill to meet my expectation?" Or, "Do they know I have this expectation of them?"

Being a good friend, spouse, partner, worker, neighbor, and person is doing what you would like others to do for you. If you do not want people to be late to your dinner party, don't be late to theirs. Your expectations are no more important than anyone else's. If people are not meeting your expectations, ask yourself, "Am I meeting other people's expectations?"

"

DO TO OTHERS AS YOU
WOULD HAVE THEM DO
TO YOU.

LUKE 6:31

"

Even if the person knew you had a reasonable expectation, that does not mean your expectation will not have to change. Some people are simply not up for the job.

If you decided to be a truck driver tomorrow, filled out the application, got in the semi-truck and headed down the road, would that make you a good truck driver? NO, because you would still need training. You need time and experience. Nevertheless, there is no guarantee. You could still be terrible. You might even get fired. You might quit and decide to be a baker instead. Finding your true talent in bagels and cupcakes. We are not made to be the best at everything.

What if you became a parent? Parenting is usually OJT (on the job training). Some people are more natural at it and have had good role models. While others never catch on and should be fired. But sending them to get another job is much more difficult, because now a child is left behind feeling unloved and unwanted.

When a person becomes a parent, it is reasonable to expect them to be a parent who will love, care, and provide for their child, guiding the child to become a healthy, functioning adult. When they do not live up to that expectation, many people are hurt. Numerous times this deep betrayal can leave people emotionally, physically, and spiritually wounded. It is a common story played out generation after generation.

How do you forgive a parent who is abusive, neglectful, or abandons a child? It is very difficult, and the situations can be tragic. The offending parents' inability to provide love comes from their own pain and experiences. This could be addiction, mental health problems, or pain they are carrying from their own childhood. Again, pain rolls downhill, to the next generation. Forgiving them does not mean what they did is okay. To forgive them means **you do not expect from them what you expected before.**

One spring afternoon, I met with a 60-year-old woman who had a long string of life problems (divorces, difficult relationships, health concerns). During our conversation, she brought up her biological father. Her father left the family when she was an infant. She never knew him and was never able to find him. She had created a fantasy of what he would have been like. But her magical thinking was so detailed that she was convinced he was out in the world somewhere, missing her. And maybe he was. But the fantasy went from war hero to loving father, and she had never spent any time with him.

After writing down her story and examining it, she could see what was true and what was fantasy. What does she know to be true? She knows that when she was born her father was there. He wanted to be a father. She has family accounts and pictures to back up the story. Her father had the will, at the time. But her father had alcohol problems along with other stability issues. As a result, he did not have the skill to be a father. That is the truth of the story. As a child, her heart wanted a healthy father to love her, and to be her protector. And as an adult, she still longed for that fatherly connection, a valid expectation.

The lack of a significant father figure affected her relationship decisions for the rest of her life. At the time of her birth, her father had hopes and dreams that he would be the father she was hoping for. That brought her joy. Examining the story helped her to see her father as a flawed individual, instead of the fantasy she had made up. She worked on forgiveness from this point.

Shifting Expectations

She shifted her perspective about the loss of her biological father. This allowed the truth of the story to bring her to gratefulness. Grateful for the other father figures in her life and those family members who showed up for her. She was not letting him off the hook for his leaving. What he did was unfair to her and wrong. What she was deciding was that forgiving him allowed her to have compassion. Compassion for the little girl that wanted her Dad, and for the addict she never knew. Forgiving him let her drop the expectation that he was a knight in shining armor out there in the world trying to get back to her. She could grieve the loss of her fantasy father, and embrace the reality that he did not have the skill to be her Dad. She no longer had the expectations of him that she once did.

If someone has been abusive towards you, your wishes and expectations are now crushed. You need to readjust. If you do not, you will find yourself back in a harmful situation with the same outcome. When someone has shattered what we expected of him or her, we tend to be stunned into inaction. We keep going, anticipating them to deliver on our original expectations.

They are warning you that they are not up for the job, whatever it is. The person is waving a bright yellow caution sign your way. Many times,  we do not believe them. We do not adjust our expectations or our boundaries. Instead, we retain our original wishes, hopes, and dreams. We keep forging ahead on our path getting our feelings hurt, missing caution signs, and blinking red lights. Finally, when we come to a full stop, we are full of un-forgiveness.

Communicating Expectations

I have five boys. Now, I don't mean to pick on the male gender, but every time I ask any of them to empty the trash, they are happy to do it. But they never automatically put a new trash bag in the trashcan. It is a little thing I know, but over the years my frustration has grown. No deep scar here, just frustration. My expectation is that when they empty the trash, they put a new bag back in. I discovered that none of my boys put a new trash bag in the trashcan because they were unaware of my expectation. As soon as I asked them, "Would you empty the trash, and when you're done would you please put in a new bag?" My problem was solved. My expectation was clearly stated and clearly understood. This is a bit of a silly example, but it shows how we go around assuming that people know exactly what we want from them. And when we don't get what we want, we walk around with our feelings hurt, not understanding why others don't care about us.

We hope and expect others to do better and to be better. When they don't, we are disillusioned and unsatisfied. Now, you are probably thinking that as a reverend I should be saying that miracles happen. Yes, miracles do happen, God can step in and change everything. Pray, and pray again. While you are doing that, please be aware that God gave you the ability to love yourself enough not to put yourself in harm's way. Love and adjust your expectations of others, so you can take yourself out of the fantasy world, and help yourself to make real life decisions.

Now it might sound like I am asking you to lower your expectations. Sure, that is the easy way out. If all your expectations are at rock bottom, no one (including yourself) can disappoint you. There would be nowhere to go but up. "Hope for the best but expect the worst," is not what I am saying. I am saying to be reasonable and balanced. Remember, we all do not have the will or the skill to meet everyone's expectations.

Here is my forgiveness story about my mom. I now recognize that my mother had the will to be a good mother. However, her issues and her pain caused her to not always have the skill to be the mom my siblings and I needed.

Forgiving Betty Tyme

My mom, Betty Tyme, had an hourglass figure, deep black hair, and large round crystal blue eyes. She was born with a talent few have, and beauty that she used skillfully. Her soulful singing voice was phenomenal. Seeing her sing live was truly a magical experience. She made singing and performing look easy. Betty Tyme knew how to work a crowd and charm any man she had in her sights. She was always the life of any party. Her life resembled a juicy novel that was set in the heyday of Hollywood, with cocktails, sex, and rumors of the Mafia.

My mother and the famous Elizabeth Taylor could have been sisters. With more than looks and talent in common, they both collected husbands. My biological father was my mom's third husband. Her total hus-

band count was six, plus one live-in boyfriend. She had five children. My twin brother and I were Mom's fourth and fifth children (15 years separated us from our closest older sibling). She did not look like she had five children. Marilyn Monroe would have envied her figure, and she knew Marilyn, along with many of the other big names back then.

After her first husband had left her, (who was the true love of her life and rumored to be in the Mafia), she fell back on her incredible singing talent, eventually earning a record contract with Dot Records. She worked at all the big clubs in Los Angeles, Palm Springs, and Las Vegas. My name, Misty, was inspired by a song. Mom was signing at the Sahara Hotel in Las Vegas when a music director for the big nightly show found out she was pregnant and said, "If you have a girl, name her Misty," after the hit song released in 1959.

At the time, Mom did not know she was carrying twins. She went along with the advice of the music director and named me Misty Tyme (Tyme was my Mother's stage name). My twin brother, John Glenn was named after our father and grandfather.

The spotlight loved Betty Tyme, following her everywhere she went; it needed her and she needed it. "I am the star," she would say. Not only was she a star on stage; she needed to be the star in every aspect of her life. If anyone or anything threatened to outshine her, it brought out my mother's dark side.

It is common for mothers and daughters to have struggles. However, my mom did not struggle, she battled. If you were not a skilled debater, it was not a good idea to tangle with her. She would detect your weakness and in a few sentences, have you willing to admit to anything out of pure fear. My mother had lifelong clashes with relatives, neighbors, and even random strangers.

Her passionate ability to argue made all of her children's lives rough. She, and whoever she was currently married to, would get into alcohol-fueled arguments that either ended with them passing out or walking out. Betty kept her children fed and clothed, but she did not manage to shield any of us from the chaos of her choices. Growing up in this type of pain, as many children do, you develop a deep resentment over the childhood you lived, and a longing for the childhood you could have lived.

One drama would pass, and then we would move on to the next adventure, or the next marriage. As a result, we would change schools and houses about every two years. All of us children always had the sense that we were in the way of her career or our next stepfather. When I was about twelve, she yelled at me, "If I had not had children I would have been a big star." I have a sense that she was right.

We knew Mom loved us, even throughout all of the chaos. Mom always made a big deal over birthdays or any holiday. Her ability to cook was legendary, and our table was always filled with warm, wholesome food. She had a hard working and adventurous spirit, which all of her children inherited.

Betty Tyme made big leaps in her life. She leaped into relationships, projects, and even businesses, feet first. Most of her leaps were uninformed jumps from a cliff. All the men she picked abused her. She had been beaten, raped, and left by the men who supposedly loved her. Always leaving her with children and no partner to rely on.

Was my mom, Betty Tyme evil? Did my mom try to hurt us because she wanted to? None of her children ever felt she was trying to hurt us. She just made seriously bad decisions. We knew we were loved, but we did not know if we were safe.

If you had the guts and nerve to ask her version of past events, you would get a very different tale. Mom was never wrong when it came to the decisions she made. She felt she was making choices that would provide for her children. These choices included marrying men whom she did not love. One of the men she married had tried to rape her best friend, but she was losing her house in a foreclosure. She needed him, or she would have been homeless. She felt that desperate.

As I grew, so did my seething resentment towards my mother and my difficult family life. During the first day of my senior year of high school, I moved out of my house. I worked two jobs and finished high school early. I had to get away from the vodka-driven quarrels that happened like clockwork every night. Surprisingly, my mom was excited for me. She helped me decorate and made sure my cabinets were full of food.

Years later, when I was married and had my first child, (her fifth of eleven grandchildren), she was supportive and helpful. My mom loved babies. The trouble would begin when the babies grew into young children. If they mentioned their other grandmother, she was instantly jealous, feeling the spotlight pulled off of her. If the kids did not notice her and tell her how pretty she was, she would exclaim that the child was a brat.

When husband number six left her after cheating with the neighbor,

Betty Tyme picked herself up again and started singing. She began singing at a local club and put out a new CD. She was 74 and still had a remarkable voice. She also found a boyfriend, and they moved in together. Her grown children were thrilled. Mom was always easier to deal with when she had romance in her life.

A few years later, the live-in boyfriend noticed some changes in her behavior. He explained that she would make plans to do something and then totally forget. When he would mention the previously made plans, she would fly off the handle accusing him of drinking too much. Soon the live-in boyfriend left because my mom's behavior had gotten more difficult than usual. The boyfriend was less abusive than my mom's six husbands, but no match for my mother's ability to disagree.

On my next visit, I went with my mom to her family practice physician. The doctor skillfully distracted her by having a nurse take her away for a test. That is when he told me he was sure she had dementia. With her musical ability, her brain had been able to hide her disease longer than normal. Even in her late seventies, she would drink two to three screwdrivers a night, heavy on the vodka, light on the orange juice. She had many head traumas from all the spousal abuse. Her poor brain was both pickled and bruised.

My mom's downward slide came fast, changing the diagnosis to Alzheimer's Dementia. Soon she could no longer live alone. My older siblings tried to help, but it became apparent that I was the one who would need to handle her care.

The next step was a locked memory care facility. I found a great facility not far from my home. It was warm and lovely. She would have her own apartment, minus a stove, as she could no longer be trusted to cook. Call me evil or a genius, but I knew I would have to lie to get her there. I told her that I had found a senior living apartment complex that was like being on a cruise ship. With a full restaurant and eligible men. I had her interest immediately. What I did not mention was she would no longer have her car or the option to cook. She would also have to give up her beloved dog.

Then we got to her new apartment. She thought the apartment was too small and she noticed the kitchen did not have a stove. I lied again and told her that this was not her permanent apartment, as they were remodeling hers. Because of her disease, she believed me. Soon, she did not notice the lack of a stove or that she never moved into her remodeled apartment. Her downhill slide accelerated.

She still had a whopper of a temper and would show it. Once she charged at me, trying to hit me because she wanted to know who stole her car. This situation was just one of the things she was angry about. Until the day came when she forgot why she was mad. That is when Alzheimer's Dementia became a blessing. You have to remember why you are mad to stay mad.

Then my mother lost the memory of almost everyone in her life, including the men who hurt her and all the regrets of lost stardom. However, she never forgot the first love of her life, the handsome Italian she married when she was just 17. (Rumor had it he had changed his name and returned to Sicily, Italy, but later we discovered he just went to Arizona.)

As her anger fell away, she truly was in the moment, because the moment was all she had. On a few occasions, she forgot that her daughter, my sister, had died of cancer. On a positive note, she also did not notice that I was watering down her vodka. Mom's nightly one or two Screwdrivers were now three-quarters watery vodka and orange juice. Her addiction to drinking was so deeply embedded that she never completely stopped.

Even while caring for her, I still held onto much of my bitterness. But I would stuff it down so I could care for her as lovingly as possible. I saw her every day. Sometimes I would be at her facility three times a day. I was in charge of all the decisions in her life. I would take her out to Sunday brunch each week and take her shopping.

My mom was still experiencing the consequences of her life decisions, even if she did not know why, anymore. Only a few of her grown children and grandchildren would visit. Other family members had a hard time even calling her. She was the poster child for how not to live your life.

One day near Christmas, when I was visiting her, she looked up at me and asked if I was Misty. I said yes. She took my hand and tears rolled down her face. She said that she loved me and she did not know who she was anymore. At that moment, she was not the lady who made such bad decisions that hurt her children; she was just a little old lady who needed me to hold her hand and tell her that I loved her.

Living in the moment with my mother allowed me to start working on forgiving her. Throughout her whole life, she strived for admiration and love. She demanded it! Now I felt sorry for the woman who never could find completeness in knowing that she was perfect just as God had made her.

I had to give up the fantasy that she would tell me how sorry she was for *all the drama she put my siblings and me through. She did not remember the pain, and she was no longer self-justifying her past. I realized I could still love her, even with all the mistakes she had made. My bitterness melted away.*

A few months later, she became ill, and her health declined rapidly. A few days before she died, she saw the love of her life, the handsome Italian first husband, although we never saw him. In a very clear voice and with determination she said, "I have to go, he has come to take me on a date." I held her hand and told her to go. I imagine her now in Heaven on a magnificent stage singing and dancing, while six husbands cheer her on.

Weddings and Funerals

When I marry a young couple, they have wishes and expectations of what their life will be. They are full of love for that perfect person standing across from them, and excitement for what their futures will hold. Maybe it's three kids, and the perfect house... Of course, their spouse will always agree with them. That is why you see smirks on the faces of married couples attending weddings. They know the truth. Committed love is not perfect. The married couples that have some years on them remember the love that brought them together, and the magic of it all. But now they know that forgiveness is another link between love and expectations. Neither of them turned out to be the fantasy that they thought they would be.

I like performing vow renewals and funerals because both have real life in them. During vow renewals, the kids are not perfectly behaved, the house has laundry strewn all over it, and each spouse knows they will not always agree. The couple understands that the dreams of the wedding day have turned into what real life looks like, and they love each other more for it. Deep committed love comes from living real life together. The family issues, work issues, deaths and illness, are part of growing together; sharing in the happy times and the difficult times.

During funerals, you find out about the life the person built or the life they missed. You see the ripple of a legacy they have cultivated. This legacy could bear sweet fruit or bitterness.

Marking the end of a life can be tricky. It is a balance, but an officiant should never lie because the family members and friends know who the person was. Have you ever been to a funeral and left saying "I don't know who they were talking about? That was not the person I knew." Are you supposed to forget that they did things or lived their life in a way that caused pain? No, you are not. But you can forgive them. Religious officiants should bring the love of God to the service. Yes, sharing the life of the person that is real, but with a dose of love. God loves the person, even if they lived a life that was difficult or sad.

Grief and Forgiveness

Death is not the only type of loss. It can be a divorce or other types of separation in a relationship. It can be the loss of your innocence during childhood. Or even a major life event, (moving, changing jobs, health issues) can cause grief. Many times, we do not put enough importance on the types of losses we go through in life. They can all cause grief and grief therapy can be helpful.

The relationship between grief and forgiveness, whether related to a person or life situation, is that you need to forgive what you hoped and expected. Then you can face the reality of who the person was or what the situation is.

When a death of a loved one happens, expected or unexpected, there are no words that can express the pain. I have often described grief as an unexpected delivery. The delivery truck shows up, drops off boxes and boxes of grief, and as the truck leaves, it runs you over. None of them are what you asked for, and you cannot return them to the sender. Over the years, you randomly get to open the grief packages. It is your grief. Grief is hard, very hard. This anguish can be compounded when you have had a difficult relationship. Grief can be a double-edged sword, sharp with sadness on one side, and never-ending loss on the other.

If you are faced with the loss of someone, along with the pain and anger of un-forgiveness, your emotions can be tumbled together. How can you miss someone you have such negative feelings for? These emotions become a mountaintop, from which I have screamed many choice words. I thought I would certainly not feel such grief for my brother when he passed. Many times in my life, I had wished he would disappear. Now he had. His death was the type of disappearing that I could not wish him back from.

The truth of the matter is, I had to grieve the relationship I did not have. The relationship I had hoped for since I was young. Sometimes, I did not even realize that I still had my childhood wish for that relationship. The dream was far down in my core. I had buried it, covering it with layers of anger and unfulfilled expectation.

We have all heard the old saying "time heals all wounds." This is a big lie that society uses to try to help us feel better. Grief is a pain that can stay a lifetime. You can recover from grief; you can. Part of recovering from grief is not just letting time go by; it is what you do with the time. Grief is a sneaky beast. It will stay for as long as you feed it.

Grief stops your world. Sorrow slows you down so much that it feels like the rest of the world is flying past you at the speed of light. When you are in grief, to do anything seems very odd. To get back "up to speed" you need to start to move forward, slowly, but moving. How do you do this when your feet are stuck in what feels like the deepest, saddest, darkest mud ever? You can start by being honest about the person you lost. Be honest about your relationship with them. If your relationship tipped towards more love than hate, be grateful. Really grateful! If your relationship was rocky with unfulfilled expectations, then work on forgiveness. In either circumstance, you can learn and grow.

> THERE IS NO GROWTH WITHOUT LOSS, NO LOSS WITHOUT GROWTH.
>
> ELIZABETH KUEBLER-ROSS

When one of my dear friends died after she fought a rare form of sweat gland cancer, I was devastated. Her death was the opposite of my brother Glenn's in every way. We had shared many happy years of friendship and fun memories. We also knew she was going to die. Glenn's death was a surprise, and we had shared a lifetime full of unhappy times. When my friend died, I grieved deeply. She was young, and her death seemed so unfair. This was another time in my life when I tried to make sense of something that felt so senseless. Eventually, her death made me profoundly grateful for all the good memories and the precious conversations I had with her. Her death was such a great loss, and out of that loss, I discovered all that I have. Her death reminded me to not take for granted friends and my happy relationships.

When Glenn died, the grief was very different, because our relationship was very different. You do not grieve every death the same. It mirrors your relationship. If you had unfulfilled expectations, then your grief will reflect that. If your relationship was loving and caring, your grief will reflect that, even through the intense sadness.

Local churches, community centers, hospitals, and hospices run support groups for grief as well. You can do the usual web searches to find them. Many are called "Grief Share." These can be helpful to share your story, your pain, and to find others who have experienced great loss. When you meet someone else who has gone through the death of a loved one, you recognize the pain. Pain that reaches so deeply only one that has felt that pain can understand. This is why going to support groups is so helpful.

Let me leave you with a closing thought about grief. At some point, each and every one of us will experience the death of someone we love. (Last time I checked, there is a 100% mortality rate.) Some people experience grief early in life; others are lucky enough not to get touched by grief until much later. When you meet someone who is grieving, please understand that his or her world has just stopped turning.

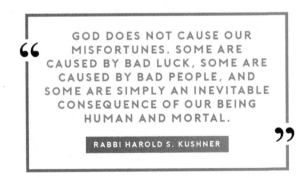

> **GOD DOES NOT CAUSE OUR MISFORTUNES. SOME ARE CAUSED BY BAD LUCK, SOME ARE CAUSED BY BAD PEOPLE, AND SOME ARE SIMPLY AN INEVITABLE CONSEQUENCE OF OUR BEING HUMAN AND MORTAL.**
>
> RABBI HAROLD S. KUSHNER

When Bad Things Happen

"Why do bad things happen to good people?" I know I have asked this question many times before, have you? Why do good things happen to bad people? If God does exist, and He is the big guy behind the gigantic clouded curtain, then why is all this senseless pain, hurt, and abuse happening down here on planet Earth? Why do kids get cancer? Why do the murderers live to a ripe old age? Why does a tornado destroy one house, while another is left untouched? These questions and many more have been asked throughout time.

If Rabbi Kushner is correct, that God is not causing all these "bad" things, then how are we to make sense out of the things that happen to us? These questions, and many more are asked in every generation. I do not think the question is ever completely answered. The best response I heard during a sermon once was brief and to the point: "We are spiritual beings having a human experience. We have free will; and we made most of the mess in this world, ourselves."

Do you ever think that God will be asking us all the same questions? Why are you hurting children? Why are you not taking care of the body given to you? Why are you fighting wars? Why are you causing so much sadness to the people you love? Why are you destroying the planet I gave you? How are we going to answer these questions?

The reality is we cannot explain why so many bad things happen. There are as many reasons as there are bad things. If we cannot blame someone or something, does that change our ability to forgive? No. As we learned in the previous chapters, forgiveness is about us. What we can do is use forgiveness as a tool to get through the bad things.

Apologies - A Good Apology and How to Make Amends

When you were examining your story, you might have found that you need to apologize for your portion of the situation. A good apology can help heal deep wounds and bridge a gap where no bridge existed before. Our egos struggle with apologizing, especially if we feel the other person is more wrong than we are.

This brings us back to the survey I mentioned earlier that shows we love an apology. (Fetzer 2010 survey on Love and Forgiveness). Often, we say we cannot forgive because the person has not apologized. This is because we still want to be right and the other person to be wrong. (Fetzer 2010 survey on Love and Forgiveness). Often, we say we cannot forgive because the person has not apologized. We still want to be right and the other person to be wrong.

We've all made mistakes big and small. We've all had to face the music, walk the line, hang our head low, and apologize. Of course, some of us are better than others at apologizing. Why is apologizing so difficult?

First, we have to say we're sorry and admit that we did something wrong. It flies in the face of human nature, our ego, and the idea that we will "lose." We are wired to win, and our egos love to be winners.

APOLOGY:
A REGRETFUL
ACKNOWLEDGMENT OF
AN OFFENSE OR
FAILURE.

AMENDS:
TO COMPENSATE OR
MAKE UP FOR A
WRONGDOING.

With maturity, we learn to own up to what we have done, and apologizing is good not only for our souls but also for others around us. We learn from our mistakes. We learn that we will not fall over from disgrace and even though we are not perfect, we are lovable. We can start over again.

There is nothing worse than knowing someone is sorry, only because they were caught with their hand in the cookie jar. We also know those certain someones whom I call, "Right Die-ers." These are the people who tell you it's sunny outside when you're standing in a rainstorm, soaking wet. No matter what evidence you give them, they refuse to own up to the truth. They'll die before they would ever admit that they were wrong. I'm going to assume you are not a "Right Die-er." Most people understand that no one is right all the time. Usually, the opposite is true. Most of us are wrong most of the time.

A good apology acknowledges the pain you have caused. It does not put the blame on the other person or situation. An apology should never include a "but." That is just telling the person that you have an excuse for what you did or said. "But I was tired that day." "But I did not know that would upset you." and the best one, "But you made me mad." That is not a personal apology. That is trying to find an excuse for your bad behavior.

A good apology helps make amends; it shows that you are trying to rebuild trust or correct what was wrong. Making amends includes fixing something, or financially paying the person back. If what you did hurt someone's reputation, then it is your responsibility to try to restore his or her reputation.

If you feel guilty, that means you have a conscious, and you are not a psychopath. Good news! But guilt is also misplaced many times. There is a simple test for guilt. Ask yourself one question when you are feeling guilty. "Did I do something wrong to someone intentionally?" If it was intentional, then apologize, make amends, and learn from your actions. Try hard not to repeat. If it was unintentional, then guilt is not appropriate. You are feeling bad because someone is upset with you, or because there is tension in a situation. Go and try to have a conversation with the other person involved, and maybe you can clear things up.

In most, not all, situations, we have contributed to the hurt feelings and misunderstandings and an apology can help to heal. But, the apology needs to be a really good one. We have all been on the receiving end of a bad apology. Those insincere words of a person getting you to forget the issue ever happened or manipulating you into admitting you are wrong.

Remember when you were a kid and your parents made you apologize after you were in trouble? Most of the time you did not have remorse for punching your brother, but you knew it got you off the hook and back to what you wanted to do. This behavior is how you started the beginning of your training in insincere apologies.

Most people have also been taught that if you told the truth and apologized right up front, your punishment would be less severe. If you own up to your indiscretion, people will more likely give you another chance. Look at our politicians and celebrities. If they stand up in front of the nation and own up to what they did, we will reelect them. We will go back to their shows, and publicly say they deserve another chance.

Everyone will make mistakes, big and small. I'm not sure if we regular people get off the hook as easily as politicians and celebrities, but taking ownership is a big part of a good apology. In the same way, if you hide away, lie, and do not take ownership of your mistakes, people will make sure you pay for it. People want to know you are truly sorry.

Usually, a good apology starts with trust. What if a person has not been reliable, and you have heard this apology before? Then, it is much harder to believe that apology this time around. When you are giving or receiving an apology, ask yourself, have you or have they worn out the apology welcome?

WORK IT QUESTIONS

Time to work on the expectations in your story. Please refer to the story you previously wrote and answer the following questions:

How did the person or situation not live up to what you expected them to do or be?

What was your hope for the person or the situation?

Was the person aware of your expectation of them? If so, what was their reaction to letting you down?

Do you think the expectation you have of the other person in this situation was reasonable? If yes, do you think they feel that your expectation was reasonable? If no, do you think they are disappointed in their ability to not fulfill this expectation?

Does the person have the WILL or the SKILL to fulfill your expectation? What are they missing to fulfill your expectation?

Do you feel unresolved grief over the situation?

How has grief affected you in your life? Are you stuck in loss?

Would you be willing to do grief work in therapy or a support group? What type of therapy are you most comfortable with?

YOUR THOUGHTS:

PREPARE
CHAPTER SEVEN

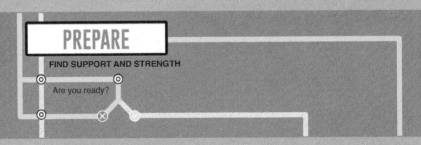

PREPARE

FIND SUPPORT AND STRENGTH

Are you ready?

STEP 3 - Prepare
Prepare to Forgive

In the last chapter, you examined your story and looked deeper into the expectations you have of others, or even of yourself. This process can be a very therapeutic exercise. You faced some new realities that the person or situation could not meet your expectations. You looked at your grief. You recognized the sadness of a relationship lost by physical distance or death. Now it is time to move onto the next step of the Forgiveness Algorithm, Prepare.

Why Prepare?

The pain that accompanies un-forgiveness can be tied in a tight knot inside of you. You might need some help to unravel it. This help can be in the form of therapy, spiritual counseling, prayer, journaling, ceremony, or support from friends. I call these, forgiveness tools.

Holding onto pain for a long time creates patterns that can be hard to let go. If I asked you to go and brush your teeth right now, you could do it without thinking. Why? Because you have been brushing your teeth for a long time (at least I hope you have). In the same way, your mind, heart, and body have formed habits when reacting to situations and people. To change these routines and truly be able to let go, you will need to do some work.

You could be in this chapter longer than any other. That is ok. You need to spend time nurturing yourself and reaching out for help. When you are using the forgiveness tools, refer to your written story and the Work It Questions whenever you need clarification and inspiration.

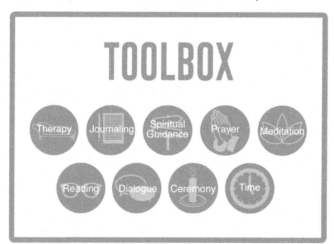

Forgiveness Tools

There are many things you can do when you are preparing to forgive. It is time to get out your Forgiveness Toolbox. I used multiple tools in my preparation for forgiving my twin brother. For me, these included spiritual guidance, therapy, reading, dialog, prayer, and ceremony.

Obviously, some situations hurt deeper than others and will need more tools. The toolbox is for you to decide what you need to help you get to the point of healing and forgiveness.

Here is a list of forgiveness tools you can use on your forgiveness journey. If you have a tool that you know works for you, add it to your toolbox.

Therapy

I am a big fan of therapy! I would not be where I am today without the well-educated, patient, loving therapists who have helped me in my life. When I was younger, I thought therapy was for the weak. I was a strong 'hear me roar,' type of woman! Why would I need therapy?

When my second marriage started to fail, my husband and I began marriage counseling. I went with one goal, I wanted the counselor to tell me I was right and he was wrong. Oh, and if she could "fix" him too, that would be great. After our very first counseling session, our counselor fired us. Yes, you can be fired from therapy. She was nice about it, but ultimately the effect was the same. Do not come back. She saw that what was needed to save our marriage went far deeper than things we could or would tackle. We were two people who were not there for the right reasons. On the way out of the door, she recommended that we each get our own therapist. She suggested to work on our own issues from our marriage. At the time, I was sure what she meant was what we both had brought into the marriage.

Ultimately, our marriage fell apart. Around the same time, I found myself having a panic attack at a stoplight. For a woman who was resilient and able to pull herself up by her bootstraps, I was falling apart at the corner of Fourth and Main, right in front of the supermarket. That's when I decided that maybe I should look into getting a therapist.

I found a therapist based on the recommendations of a friend. When I walked in, I proudly announced, "Nice to meet you. I agree to five visits. I don't want to talk about my childhood, as that has nothing to do with my present situation." The very nice middle-aged, organically dressed therapist looked at me and gave me a little smile as she asked me to sit down.

Little did I know that the next six months in therapy would change my life. Eventually, we did talk about my childhood, my alcoholic parents, my loveless first marriage, my difficult second marriage, and the deaths of my father and my sister.

I learned that therapy had nothing to do with being weak. It was about being strong enough to share my heart and pain with a person who has been trained to be my life's referee. This referee was not taking sides. She was not emotionally connected to my past. She could see through my stories, as broken as they were. She could see how they had formed my life choices, both good and bad. I finally gained clarity and started to heal.

Years later, I went back to therapy to help deal with the grief I was feeling after the death of my dear friend, older brother, and my mother. Yes, if you are counting, my older sister, older brother, twin brother, mother, father, and best friend have all died. This list does not include the patients that I have gotten to know who have touched my soul. Grief has been a deep dark well that I have drawn from many times.

Therapy helped me with my forgiveness work, and to bring me through my grief. I still go to a therapist for tune-ups, because life can be tough and everyone can benefit from a life referee.

How long will you have to go to therapy if you are working on a forgiveness issue? I wish I could give you that answer. Every situation and every person are different. What is important is that you find a therapist that can partner with you as you work through your forgiveness journey.

 Why journal? Journaling can be used as a lifelong tool to help you know yourself better. Some people keep a daily journal. Some people's journal is a mix of daily to-dos with a blend of thoughts, quotes, and things they must express. When we were kids, we called it our diary. Journaling is more about your soul than it is about your grocery list.

To help show the power of journaling, I have added the story of my dad's battle with cancer. Journaling my thoughts and emotions through the entirety of this roller coaster ride was one way I was able to begin moving through my grief into healing. I still have the journal I kept when my adopted dad died 20 years ago.

George – Not my Father, but my Dad

My dad had smoked from the time he was 12 years old (smoking rolled corn silk in the fields of Iowa). He had stopped smoking eleven years before he was diagnosed with esophageal cancer. However, the damage had already been done to the deep layer of cells in his esophagus. The time from the diagnosis to his death was just a short, intense six months. My dad died just three months after my sister lost her battle with metastatic breast cancer.

My dad adopted me when I was ten years old. We used to say; he picked me. He was not my biological father. That was the man who made me and left. This man was dad. My parents had a rocky abusive relationship, yet amidst the chaos, he was still able to be my dad.

He was far from perfect; he was no TV dad for sure. He suffered deep pain left from a very sad childhood. When he ten years old, he was dropped off at a farm with a childless couple after his parents had died. His adopted father beat him and treated him like a farm hand, not a son. He rarely spoke about his childhood, until he was dying. He longed to know the parents he barely remembered.

I walked into his hospital room on a rare sunny day in Portland, Oregon, as he was preparing to go for another radiation treatment. He had already endured numerous treatments that caused deep burning on his throat, leaving him with what looked like the worst sunburn you have ever seen. However, this sunburn was not just on his skin. It reached deep inside of his throat, forming blisters that ran to the 9-centimeter long tumor that the doctors were trying to kill. He was not able to sip the smallest bit water. He was six feet tall and weighed only 110 lbs.

As I came into his room I found him sitting in a wheelchair looking frail. I tried to sound upbeat as I said "Hi Dad, are you ready to go to your radiation treatment?" In a small voice he said, "I am done." Just three words, "I am done." I knew immediately what he was referring to. He was done with treatment. I instantly clarified, "Do you know what this means?" He nodded his head, "yes." Just as he finished the movement of his head at the end of the yes, the nurse walked in. She was ready to take him down to radiation oncology for his treatment. I instantaneously blurted out, "He is not going." I felt very protective. The nurse stopped immediately. I told her what my dad had decided. She turned to my dad and confirmed his decision. My dad died a month later.

When I read that 20-year-old journal, I am transported back to that time in my life. Yes, it was a very sad time. Tears form in my eyes as I read about caring for my dad as he withered away. However, it is also a treasured time.

So much forgiveness, love, and thankfulness were expressed during those months.

In that journal, I also wrote about the deep grief I was working through after losing my dad and my sister just three months apart. The despair is spread all over the pages. What do I feel now when I read those miserable pages? I feel relief. Relief that I am not there anymore; and, more importantly, I feel strong. I have survived that pain and I can be happy again.

Your journal is you on paper. You can see your inabilities, your strength, your growth, and most importantly, where you have overcame tough situations. It is also a good place to write what you cannot say, or should not say, to someone in person. In today's world of email, there is no pause button. Write it down first and check your reaction. Are you being true to yourself, or are you reacting from pain? This is another good place to write yourself honest.

When journaling, you do not have to follow any rules; it is your journal. You can draw pictures or use colored pencils. Anything you want. Write as little or as much as you want. It is for you. You could start your journaling with a question. Here are examples of some good questions to start: What am I thankful for today? What do I want to change in my life? If I could do anything in the world what would it be?

I wish I could forget the time I

because

What is the biggest lesson I have learned in my life so far?

Keep your journals so that you can randomly go back and read them. The insight you express will surprise you.

Before licensed therapists became popular, the only person you went to talk to in confidence was your local priest, rabbi or pastor. These were the local village specialists you turned to with issues and needed advice. Their counsel would come with a dose of theology, and, usually, common sense. As the world moved towards the science of the brain, psychiatrists and psychologists became more prevalent. Studying human behavior and the diseases of the brain became key in understanding why we do what we do.

The world has come back around to the understanding that science and our spiritual needs are interlocked. It is a short trip from the head to the heart, about 16 inches. Spiritual teachers help us answer questions such as, "What can I learn from this?" and "Where does God fit into my life?" However spiritual teachers do have limitations. They do not treat clinical mental health illnesses. Those issues should be handled by a psychiatrist or a psychologist.

Working with a spiritual counselor is not the same as having therapy with a licensed therapist or psychiatrist. Spiritual counseling or guidance work refers to working with your clergy, leaders of your church, a spiritual counselor, or a life coach. In today's landscape, you have many choices.

Spiritual counseling offers you a chance to merge your head, heart, and soul. Not just working out why you are in your situation, but taking into account your spiritual journey. Frequently prayer or meditation is included in spiritual counseling.

There are different degrees of education, ordinations, and certifications when it comes to spiritual counselors and life coaches. It is up to the consumers to educate themselves on who they are seeing. There are specialists in many different types of alternative therapy, from Drum Therapy (yes, you get to bang a drum), Spiritual Counseling, Reiki, and Hypnosis. What you need to decide is whether you are comfortable with it and what your bank account can afford. Most alternative therapy is not covered by insurance. Some churches do offer free counseling services. I strongly suggest that you look into their references. In all cases, make sure the provider has a confidentiality policy, and that they stick to it.

Prayer

Prayer takes many forms. When I first went to seminary, I was surprised when I sat next to a fellow student who said they had never prayed except in church, and only in a formal recited prayer. My experience with prayer has been much more casual; more like, "Hey God, how are things? Let's talk." After my fellow seminarian had told me their polite type of prayer, I was worried that I was rude to God. I thought I should take on a more formal approach. By the end of my schooling, I was pleased to learn about many other forms of prayer. From the "hey dude" conversational prayer to the whirling dervish physical praying that combines dancing and singing.

We can meditate, contemplate, recite a mantra, or sit silently. God loves all prayers. Dress them up or dress them down. God, the Angels, and the Saints can't wait to hear from you. Pray from your heart and listen with your soul.

Prayer is communication, spoken and unspoken. When you are with a dear friend, engaged in a deep conversation, you know they are listening to every word you say. They are paying attention to every move you make, intently watching every one of your tears fall. They are comforting you by just being there. That is because they love you and want to help you. God is that friend, listening and watching as you pray.

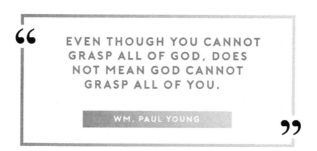

" EVEN THOUGH YOU CANNOT GRASP ALL OF GOD, DOES NOT MEAN GOD CANNOT GRASP ALL OF YOU.

WM. PAUL YOUNG

"

Even if you do not believe that prayer is a direct cell tower to the almighty God, unburdening yourself has long since been considered therapeutic. If you still struggle with deciding if your prayers are being heard and answered, put them to the test. Pray and pray again, every single day. Keep a prayer journal and write down your prayers. Over time, you will see how your prayers have been answered, or not answered. Keep in mind; no answer is also the answer. Sometimes we ask, or even beg God to give us something we think we need or want. If God just handed over your desire, it might not be good for you or the person you are praying for. God has the long-term view for your life, your loved one's life, and every creature on earth. You must trust in Him.

Prayers can be long or short. One of the shortest prayers in the Bible is when Peter, Jesus' disciple, was on a sinking boat. "Lord, save me!" It was short and to the point. However, you do not have to pray only when you are sad, scared, or under stress. You could simply check in with God and thank Him for the beauty of the day. God is right there, waiting for us to pray, forgive, and love.

I advise that you pray in a way that is comfortable for you. You may prefer to have a conversation with God while walking in nature, sitting in your car, or finding a group to pray with (church, temple, or a small group prayer circle). You can use a mantra, prayer beads, pre-written prayers, prayer book, or you can sit in silence. Prayer is part of your relationship with God. Communicate in a way that is most true to your heart.

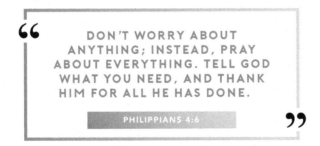

> **" DON'T WORRY ABOUT ANYTHING; INSTEAD, PRAY ABOUT EVERYTHING. TELL GOD WHAT YOU NEED, AND THANK HIM FOR ALL HE HAS DONE.**
>
> **PHILIPPIANS 4:6 "**

Jewish

A Jewish prayer said at bedtime can be found in the Siddur.
We proclaim:

"I forgive all those who may have hurt or aggravated me either physically, monetarily, or emotionally, whether unknowingly or willfully, whether accidentally or intentionally, whether in speech or in action, whether in this incarnation or another, and may no person be punished on account of me..."

Muslim

In the name of Allah, the Beneficent the Merciful.

O Allah forgive my sins of which You are aware and if I repeat it then forgive me again. O Allah! I couldn't get an opportunity to fulfill the covenants done against my evil deeds, forgive these sins too. O Allah forgive the sins done by the action of eyes, mistake of the lips, negligence of the heart, and by the movement of the tongue.

Christian

Matthew, 6:9-13 NIV
This, then, is how you should pray:
Our Father in heaven,
hallowed be your name,
your kingdom come,
your will be done,
on earth as it is in heaven.
Give us today our daily bread.
And forgive us our debts,
as we also have forgiven our debtors.
And lead us not into temptation
but deliver us from the evil.
For Thine is the kingdom,
The power,
And the glory, forever,
Amen.

Hindu

From Yajur Veda
May my body become pure.
May I be free from impurity and sin.
May I realize myself as the light divine.
May my mind become ever pure.
May my self become pure.
May I realize my self as the light divine.

Meditation is a scary word if you have never tried it. Meditation is also a buzzword in today's culture. Even the mainstream spirituality groups are jumping in on the benefits of meditation. In prayer, it is common to hear the word "contemplation." Contemplation is a synonym for meditation, or deep reflective thought. Whether you call it meditation or contemplation, it is not just for the yogis sitting in lotus position on the mountaintops anymore. Meditation and contemplation are for you. It is a gift you can give your busy thought-filled mind.

Many hospitals and medical programs are showing the benefits of meditating every day. The word meditation is a blanket term used for everything from being mindful in the moment, prayer, or sitting in silence while using a mantra to clear your mind of all thoughts. Why would you do this? Why not just take a nap? I used to say the same thing, as I am a go go go kind of person. I cannot sit still long enough to clear my mind of anything except to imagine what I should be doing next. Meditation is a break from all that go go go and a reset for your brain. Meditation is not a loss of control or mental gymnastics. Meditation is a way to give us mental contentment, peace, and a way to slow the constant activity in our brains. Meditation reduces stress in our bodies and ultimately increases our focus. Who does not want that?

How do I meditate? I hear this question often, and I used to ask the same thing. There are many ways to learn to meditate. What works for me might not work for you. You can find different types of meditation that do not require you to sit on a floor, cross-legged in a room full of other people breathing deeply. I am better with guided meditation and prayer. Some people love pure silent meditation, but for me, I call that a nap! I have included a few websites that might help you. You can also download apps on your phone, including those that are geared towards your specific faith. YouTube is a great place to find meditations. You can play them, sit back, close your eyes, and let them take you away.

Forgiveness Meditation - *Turn into Your Heart*
Rev. Misty

- Sit in a comfortable place, with no outside distraction.
- Take three deep cleansing breaths.
- Close your eyes and repeat three times, "Let me turn into my heart."
- Take another deep cleansing breath.
- Slowly bring into your mind, the person or situation you want to forgive.
- Notice whatever fear or anger comes up.
- Take a deep cleansing breath. On the out breath, feel your anger and fear soften.
- Repeat three times ... "Let me turn into my heart."
- Take a cleansing breath.
- Repeat three times ... "I choose to forgive you for whatever you may have done that has caused me pain, intentionally or unintentionally."
- Take a deep cleansing breath.
- Repeat three times ... "I release you from my expectations."
- Take a deep cleansing breath.
- On the out breath, feel your expectations of the person fall away.
- Repeat three times ... "I dissolve into the power of forgiveness."
- Take a deep cleansing breath.
- Again, visualize the person or situation you want to forgive, let them go on their way.
- Take a deep cleansing breath.
- Now gently bring into your mind and heart the image of yourself in peace (however that looks to you).
- Breathing deeply, stay in your image of peace as long as you need to.
- As you feel yourself returning to the present moment, whisper lightly, "Let it be."

Remember when you were a kid and the reading bug bit you? The words formed pictures in our mind, and new ideas would come flooding in. You understood the power of a good book. Turn off all the electronic noise and go back to that. Become a student again, but major in your life.

There is so much to read and not enough time. Have you been to the self-help section in the bookstore? You can get help on any subject, including forgiveness. Find a book (and I hope this is one of them) that touches you, makes you think, and helps you take a step forward in your life.

When I was in my early thirties, on my way to a business conference, I picked up a book in an airport newsstand that changed my life. The book is called *Everyday Grace* by Marianne Williamson. I looked at the cover, flipped to the back, and decided it looked interesting enough for the plane ride. When I started reading the book, it felt like I was the only person Marianne was writing to. I needed that book then, and I still need that book, now, almost twenty years later. When you are in need, let other people who have gone through what you are going through help you to heal. Let the wise sages and teachers teach you.

Research the sacred texts from around the world and explore how big God is. Explore your own faith's scriptures and feel the source of your inner spirit. If that seems too daunting with all those parables, poems, thees, and thous, pick up a reference guide. *The Bible for Dummies* is a great read. I own one for every religion. They sit on my bookshelf, right next to deep theological books.

After I had graduated from the seminary, I was feeling pretty shiny. I thought I knew all I needed to let go of past pain. I had come up with a plan to tell my twin brother Glenn, "I forgive you for being controlling, abusive, and mean!" I had envisioned him crying and saying thank you as he admitted all his wrongdoings. The truth is, Glenn would have looked at me and immediately become defensive. Who wouldn't?

What did my ego want? It wanted an "I am sorry." I still wanted to be right. I was not in the right place for a conversation. I did not own up to the times I had not been very nice over the years. I had always been great at talking badly about him. I had not taken into consideration his deep pain of addiction or the abuse he had suffered as a child. I blamed him for not rising above our childhood. This conversation would have ended in a verbal bashing, exactly like all the other times I tried to tell Glenn how wrong he was, and how right I was.

What would have happened if I turned the conversation around? How do you think the conversation would have gone if I had started out with, "Glenn, I want to apologize for all the times I did not treat you with respect. Or the moments when I should have been more loving to you." I suspect it would have turned an accusatory conversation into a healing conversation. There is never a guarantee on how others will act. You can only decide how you want to respond. Please decide if you have done enough work and if you are truly ready to have a conversation that can promote healing. You have a lot to think about before you decide to have this conversation.

QUESTIONS TO ASK YOURSELF:

WHAT IS YOUR GOAL OF THE CONVERSATION?

CAN YOU HAVE A CONVERSATION WITH THE PERSON WITHOUT LOSING YOUR TEMPER?

IS IT SAFE TO BE IN THE ROOM WITH THE PERSON?

DO YOU NEED TO APOLOGIZE FOR SOMETHING YOU DID?

DO YOU WANT TO HAVE A FURTHER RELATIONSHIP?

IS IT BETTER TO CUT YOUR LOSSES AND MOVE ON?

ARE YOU READY TO NOT GET AN APOLOGY?

Do you still want to have the conversation? Yes or No?

If yes, I trust that you want to do it for all the right reasons. Remember that the conversation is about clarification, not confrontation. Your goal is to have a healthy relationship with the person.

Are you ready to apologize for your part without an expectation from the other person to apologize to you? Yes, even if the other person is immoral, unethical, and just plain wrong. So, hard, right?

Now that is cleared up, let's put some guidelines in place before you go knocking on their door with a plate of cookies and a smile. You know the person you are going to talk to. You know yourself, and your triggers. Don't put yourself in a place that could make them go off. Be in your best place.

Here is a big hint! Do not put on your "I have an announcement face" and say, "I have been working on forgiving you." People tend to get a bit defensive. It is human nature rearing its ugly head.

Yes? You still want to go ahead with the conversation, and you feel ready... then go for it! You are ready to go in with a warm heart, to clarify the situation, and to have an apologize-for-what-you-did conversation. I hope it goes great.

If your answer is No, then you have figured out that a conversation is not a good idea in this situation. Good for you. Many people do not figure that out. They charge in with unrealistic hopes and expectations, only to be hurt again. If you saved yourself the pain, you just got some more of your power back. You can still forgive a person without having a conversation with them.

 Our society loves ceremony. We have ceremonies for everything from sporting events to school graduations. We use ceremonies to mark the beginnings and endings in our lives, whether small or large. Using ceremony in the forgiveness process can be extremely powerful. I have listed a few ceremonies you can try. You can also design your own. Do what feels right in your heart.

Candle Lighting Ceremony

Find a candle with a scent that resonates with you. As you light the candle, start with a prayer, welcoming God into your space. Close your eyes and think of the person you are trying to forgive. See the issue, anger, or pain they have caused you as a dark round marble right next to them. Put all your anger and pain into that marble. You might even see this marble grow as you transfer the pain into it. Now, imagine the big dark marble rolling away, far away. Envision the person who caused it staying there, not causing you any pain at all. Just standing there.

Breathe in and out. If you need more marbles, fill them up and keep rolling them away. As you end your time, you can say a prayer or add a meditation. Open your eyes when you are ready. See the warm flame of the candle. Breathe deeply, in and out. You can sit there for as long as you need to. When you are ready, blow out the candle.

Essential Oils

Essential oils are what give plants their characteristic smell. The oils are made up of small organic molecules that can change from solid or liquid to gas. Each oil and combination of oils is used in a wide variety of applications. Some oils are used for their antimicrobial and anti-inflammatory benefits while others are soothing in aromatherapy. Essential Oils are natures nurturing supportive treatment.

You can use a diffuser or you can dab a drop of the oil onto your skin. Check that the oil you choose is safe for your skin and dilute as needed. Use it during your meditation, before you sit down to pray, or in a ceremony similar to the candle.

Letter Writing Ceremony

This type of letter writing is for you and you only. Note: The letter you write is not to be sent. Never-ever.

In our family, if a letter arrived for my mother from another family member, it was usually someone telling her how she had hurt them deeply. To my mother, getting a letter meant a declaration of war. The letter was waved around the house like a flag while she rounded up the troops. As a child, I never understood why my mother received one of these letters randomly. However, when I grew up, I understood perfectly and had contemplated sending one myself. Nonetheless, I knew that no letter, no matter how well crafted, would change how my mother navigated her relationships. The letter writer would eventually have to apologize for sending the letter and lie low for a good year or so.

When writing a letter, you are writing for the same reasons you wrote your story at the beginning of this book, but in a letter, you get to be more personal. Say all the deeply personal things you want to say to the person. The good, the bad, and the hideously ugly. Pour it out. And while you are at it, have a good ugly cry. When you are done, you have a few choices:

You can read it to a very trusted person who is okay following some rules. They are not allowed to make any comments. They are not allowed to touch you – not one hug or even a pat on the hand – until you have completely finished reading the letter. Then and only then, may the person give you a hug or a pat on the hand.

If you did not do step 1, that is fine. Just read it aloud to yourself, looking in a mirror if possible. Then, when you are done, give yourself some lovely self-compassion. Cry, and forgive yourself for being angry or lashing out.

Destroy the letter. You can shred it, burn it, put it in the mud and stomp on it... whatever it takes so that you will never be able to read it again.

Written, read, and said.

Please repeat this as much as you like. You can write a pile of letters. What is important is that you are saying what you want to say to the person or people that hurt you. You can even write a letter to a situation. Tell the cancer how much you despise what it did to your life. Regardless of the situation, write down how it changed your life.

Day In Court Exercise

Your day in court exercise is similar to the letter writing exercise, with a bit more performance. This is sometimes called the "empty chair" exercise. Occasionally we just want to be heard. Many times, we do not get to have a conversation with the person who hurt us because it would not be safe, would not help the situation, or the other person has died. In this exercise, you can have your chance. You can have your "day in court." You get to be heard.

Have you ever been really angry with a person and found yourself stomping around the house, maybe shaking your fists in the air? When we are angry, we can physically feel it. If we were in a court of law, we would sit in the witness chair and tell the judge, jury, and the defendant how we have been wronged. This lets all the facts be heard, and our heart be unburdened. That is what this exercise can do for you without the big attorney bill.

First, place two chairs across from each other. In one of the chairs, tape a piece of paper with the name of the person with whom you are upset.

Now, take a seat in the opposite chair. This empty chair is creating a safe space for you to say anything and everything you want to say. So, let the chair have it! Use colorful language, put on your angry face, do whatever you need to do to let the person know how upset you are.

One more step, take your chair and move it next to the empty chair. Now you are sitting next to the person that hurt you. (Sitting next to a person is less confrontational than sitting across from them.) In a softer kinder voice, tell the empty chair what you wanted from them. What you wanted from the relationship; your expectations of them.

You might find that here your anger is less, and your sadness over the situation has come bubbling up. It is OK to cry, and it is OK to feel sad. Put your hand on the empty chair. If you want to apologize for anything, now is the time. If you want to say goodbye to the person, now is the time.

Finally, when you feel you have said all there is to say, take some deep cleansing breaths. Feel all that anger and sadness leave. You have spoken it. Now take the paper with the name of the person, from the opposite chair, tear it up and throw it away. You have said what you needed to say. Great job!

 Time is a great thing because it gives you distance from the situation. The old adage, "time heals all wounds" as I mentioned before, is crap! Time does not heal all wounds. Time helps you in a few ways, but it does not heal. It is what you do with the time that helps you to heal.

I have met people who lost a loved one twenty-five years ago, and their feelings are still as raw as the day the person died, maybe even worse. This is because during the twenty-five years, the grief, sadness, and anger have been growing. They have been feeding the sadness and anger. You have to decide to feed things that will help you heal. If you choose not to do anything about the anger and pain, it will not get better.

Time does give us perspective, because we are able to see that life is ever changing. Flowing from sad to happy and back again. Maybe that is where the famous line; "wisdom is wasted on the old" comes from. We finally figure out that letting things go is better than holding on. For many, by the time they figure this out, we are too old to do much about it. Such is the path of wisdom.

WORK IT QUESTIONS

1. What Forgiveness Tools do you feel you want to use to help you forgive?

2. What have you used in the past to help you feel better? Will it help in your situation now?

3. What could you do in the next 30 days to help you heal?

YOUR THOUGHTS:

FORGIVE

CHAPTER EIGHT

STEP 4 - Forgive
Forgiveness is a Choice

You can decide to forgive now or not. It is your decision. Forgiveness is
both decisional and emotional. You do not have to forgive anyone or anything. You can keep the ill feelings you currently have, if you choose.

You have reached the moment to decide. Are you ready to forgive?
Yes, Maybe, or No.

Yes, you might have already made the decision to forgive during your time in the Prepare chapter, or when you examined your story and discovered the person could not or would not meet your expectations. Not always an easy decision. You did so much emotional and even physical work to get to that YES.

Maybe, you have forgiven just a little bit. You might not be ready to forgive fully. A big "maybe," might be flashing in your head. Totally normal. We want to let things go, but there can still be that little pebble of un-forgiveness left rolling around in our hearts. I understand. Very normal, and in problematic situations you might have to go through the steps again. Each time will be easier, and you will be able to move faster.

No, you are still holding tight onto what happened and what should have happened. You feel like you just cannot let go. You need to do more forgiveness work. Go back to the Prepare chapter. What do you need more of to help you let go? Therapy, grief work, or some more time to process all you have learned? Whatever it is you need, go get it. I do not want you to waste another moment of your precious life all snarled up in un-forgiveness.

DON'T WAIT TO BE A LAST MINUTE FORGIVER OR YOU WILL WASTE YOUR LAST MINUTE.

Let's jump ahead many years from now when you are on your deathbed. News flash: you will die. That's blunt, I know, but I have statistics to back up the claim of a 100% mortality rate. I can assure you right now that those ugly emotions of un-forgiveness and regret will follow you to your deathbed. There was a study published in 2014, "Nurses Responses to Requests for Forgiveness at the End of Life," in the Journal of Pain and Symptom Management. The study asked 339 hospice nurses from five different countries questions about forgiveness and patient care. Nurses saw patient after patient express suffering and remorse over things they did or things others did to them during their lives. The study backs up the need to forgive right now, rather than when you are at death's door.

Good news. The study also showed that when forgiveness issues were resolved, the person's end of life had a higher quality. And after the death of the loved one, the friends' and family members' grief was easier than if they were left with un-forgiveness issues. I expect that your mom has always told you to wear clean underwear in the case of an accident. I'm going to add, "Wear clean underwear and forgive daily."

Even if you are still at no or maybe, that is exactly where you should be. You are on your specific journey. Each situation will take you down different beaten paths.

Self-Forgiveness

Why did I wait until this far into the book to cover the topic of self-forgiveness? Often, we have so much anger and pain towards others that it is hard to see the pain we have towards ourselves.

When I started to take accountability for my actions (the unkind way in which I treated my brother and talked badly about him), I felt very guilty for what I had done. I tried to justify my pain by highlighting his bad behavior. I choose my behavior. He did not cause me to act the way I did. Yes, I own it. I was not my best self. I wanted to teach him a lesson, and get some sweet revenge. Self-forgiveness was the only way I could get to a better place and to resolve the guilt I carried.

How do you forgive yourself for a behavior you are not proud of? After talking to many people, I was relieved to find out I am not the only one with this dilemma. We all make unintentional mistakes and bad decisions. These decisions hurt others; and, when we realize the pain we caused, we feel rotten. We can apologize, and maybe the person will forgive us. However many times, trust is also lost.

What do we do with our own sense of guilt and shame?

Shame is what we do to ourselves and blame is what we do to others. When we are in the middle of the shame game, it is hard for us to get ourselves out of the loop. Even when someone lets us off the blame train with full forgiveness, we can keep playing the internal shame game. Why? Because we feel we deserve it. We start mounting a case in our heads about why we are so very bad. The recurring loop we play in our heads says, "You are what you do, what you did was wicked, you must be a horrible person." Numerous people use this thinking to justify more unhealthy or hurtful actions, which causes people to keep blaming, and the internal shame continues.

You are not supposed to forget your mistakes, remember it's God's safety net. Instead, learn from your mistakes and try not to repeat. You are supposed to stop beating yourself up over them. Newsflash! No one is perfect. Just like the people you are working on forgiving, you need to have compassion for yourself. Follow the Forgiveness Algorithm for yourself. It really works.

Start by apologizing and, if possible, make amends. It can be the beginning of reconciling relationships and healing of wounds. Help yourself by learning from the situation. The biggest gift of mistakes is what you learn from them. This is a character building moment!

Remember when we went over apologies? What was the proof of a good apology? Do not repeat... I repeat, do not repeat the mistake.

We all put degrees of blame and shame on our own scales according to our beliefs and experiences. Remember, what one person finds unforgivable, another person might see as forgivable. We might not be able to forgive ourselves for the smallest of mistakes even though we would forgive others for the same or bigger offenses. No one is harder on you than you. I made a list in my head to prove I was a terrible person. When I changed my perception, I saw myself as a person who needed to be forgiven. I was so sorry for my actions, and I learned from them. I am trying really hard not to repeat them. You can do the same.

> **"**
> YOU WANT TO
> PERFORM A MIRACLE,
> FORGIVE YOURSELF.
>
> RUNE LAZULI
> **"**

Family Forgiveness

I have shared a few stories about my family. We have many more that would cause readers shock, and other people would think I had it better than they did. So many people have gone through pure horror at the hands of people who were supposed to love them. Often, I could not see the blessings in my family, because I was so angry that God had given me this family. I would fantasize that I must have been switched at birth with some other three pound twin girl, and my real family was out there somewhere. But that was just a dream. This was definitely the family I had been born into, and today I am very thankful.

During the writing of this book, I talked to my older siblings, my nephew, and Glenn's widow, about our experiences we all had with Glenn. We also discussed my mother, the fathers who left us, and the stepfather who stayed. We all have wide-ranging experiences that have affected all of our lives in both negative and positive ways. Some family members have been able to overcome the bad things they lived through. Others have not. Many of us have repeated the cycle of generations of pain we experienced.

Family is where we begin our life. Our parents, siblings, and cousins are our first friends, influences, and teachers. When you grow up in a tumultuous unhealthy family, it is hard to "un-learn" unhealthy behaviors. When the people you are supposed to trust are the people that hurt or abuse you, your brain and heart get tangled up between anger and love. Irrational becomes your normal.

Family forgiveness is about forgiving your parents, their parents, and so on, right down to the roots of your family tree. Then it's about deciding to change how the next branch will grow. You have the choice and power to stop the quintessential core of the pain. You can craft your own life. You have the control. Forgiveness gives you the power to decide how you will live; and what you teach the next generation.

If you had a crappy childhood, then make it better for your children. If you had an abusive parent, family member, or spouse, it is your choice to not repeat the abuse. Decide to forgive so you can do better and be better. It is within your power to stop the madness. Give the next generation a chance to live happier and healthier lives. Let forgiveness be your legacy.

Chapter 8: Forgive

> **"**
> IF YOU FORGIVE ANYONE'S
> SINS, THEY ARE FORGIVEN.
> IF YOU DO NOT FORGIVE THEM,
> THEY ARE NOT FORGIVEN.
>
> JOHN 20:23
> **"**

103

When I Said Yes
Forgiving Glenn, Forgiving Myself

My final decision to forgive my twin brother happened at about 4 p.m. on a sunny San Diego afternoon. I was sitting in a parking lot outside my local grocery store. My car was parked in the shade of a palm tree. Why was I sitting in the car, surrounded by all my groceries and the smell of rotisserie chicken? Because right after I had loaded the groceries into my SUV, I tossed my purse in the passenger seat and watched it spill everywhere... lipstick, wallet, receipts, and sunglasses hit the floor as my cell phone hit the dash. As I gathered up the contents and piled everything back in my purse, I grabbed my cell phone and the screen lit up. My eyes widened as I blinked at the date. My gut twisted into a knot as I murmured to a car full of groceries, "It has been two months since my twin brother died."

I had thought about Glenn each day since he died, which is typical grieving behavior. When someone you care about dies, your mind becomes a fog of thoughts. Your everyday is snarled with thoughts, memories, and reflections on what you should have said or done with that person. That day, my brain was clearer, the fog was starting to lift. Then in one swoop, my brain was all tangled again. It had been two months since my brother had died. My stomach flipped, as my mind immediately returned to the moment I learned that he had died, then to a random childhood memory, and finally to a flash of his funeral. How does our mind move so fast, like someone shuffling a deck of cards, dealing us random memories?

Grief had just delivered another dented, well-taped package for me. I looked around, half expecting to see a shadowy figure dressed in matching shorts and shirt pulling away in one of those large delivery vans marked Grief Express. Grief is sneaky like that. It will send you a delivery when you least expect it. It is one thing to open up deep emotions of grief in the privacy of your own home where no one can witness you falling apart, however, I was falling apart in the middle of a very public parking lot. At that moment, I was even more thankful for the shade of my palm tree to reduce the chances of anyone seeing me in my full-blown "ugly cry."

As I sat there, I felt deep guilt and shame rising in my gut as I thought about the last time I had seen my brother. I asked myself that simple question, "Did I do something wrong to feel guilty about?" The answer was an easy "yes," I had not treated my brother very well. Okay, "not well" was

104

putting it mildly.

I had not seen Glenn since our Mother had died. It was during our high school reunion, and I was distant and irritated with him. It would have been easy to avoid him if we had gone to one of those enormous high schools. But my little high school class of 1985 only had thirty-five people in it. When Glenn showed up I barely acknowledged him, because I was angry with him for recent events around our mom's passing. I wore my lifelong disappointment in him like an angry wool coat, making me itch with resentment. Glenn and I had a few short conversations, but that was all. I hadn't noticed when he left the reunion. I did not even say goodbye. That was the last time I ever saw my twin brother. He died later that month.

I know how grief works. It had invited me to the grief party before. I had danced this dance with its dips and spins. Grief sadness is different than any other sadness you will ever feel. To add to the layers of sadness, I also had an extra layer of un-forgiveness for my brother; the pain and anger of expectations unfulfilled. He had hopes and dreams for himself. I had hopes and dreams for our relationship. Glenn did not have the skill to maneuver through life's trials. He struggled with mental issues and physical pain. He carried the scars of a young life that had suffered abuse, and the pain of knowing he had repeated that same cycle. And add to that a scoop of addiction! Did he still have a choice to change the legacy of abuse? Yes, he did, and I am saddened he did not have the strength to make better choices. He did not stop the repeated cycle of pain, and in my own pain, I lashed out. I had a new clarity about the part I played in our relationship. How I longed to apologize for my part in it all. At that moment, as I sat in the car, tears running down my face from grief, I realized I could have been a better human being.

Through the tears, my heart, mind, and soul gave up – gave up carrying that pain. This pain had been waiting for someone else to fix it with an apology, or for someone with a magic wand to make it all better, when I had the power to fix it the whole time. In that instant, I chose to forgive Glenn for the pain he had caused me. Sitting there in the parking lot with the smell of the rotisserie chicken invading my nostrils, I forgave my twin brother. It was my choice. It was so simple, but at the same time so hard. I had gone through a great deal to reach that point. I understood that the choices he had made in his life were not okay for my life. "His life, his path," was like a repeated mantra in my mind. I did not have control over his life, yet I still felt sad thinking about how his life had turned out.

Forgiving him did not mean I would not be sad over the situation. But what I have now is freedom from the expectations I put on him, and empathy. After a few deep breaths, I wiped my eyes and drove home. I unloaded the groceries and cooked my family dinner. Okay, I warmed up the rotisserie chicken!

That night I continued thinking about my brother. Grief was still stepping all over my heart, but un-forgiveness had left. Anger had left. The place that used to hold un-forgiveness now held gratitude and empathy. I had survived a painful childhood, and I was grateful I had a twin brother. It was my choice to stop the cycle of repeated pain. I chose to change my perspective. I chose to separate from the pain and find reasons to be grateful. Forgiveness has given me a new focus. I can love Glenn, and others in my life, without agreeing with their actions. I can step back and see them as children of God. Like opening a clenched fist, I released the idea of control; not that I ever really had it in the first place.

Later that night, my husband asked me how my day was, in passing, as was usual for us. I casually looked up at him as I was putting the dishes in the dishwasher and I said, "Today I chose to forgive Glenn!" He gave me a hug. The decision to forgive Glenn has had unforeseen ripples in my life. It has helped me become more passionate about the subject of forgiveness and its life-changing effects.

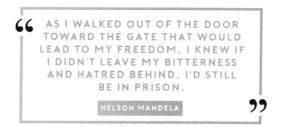

> AS I WALKED OUT OF THE DOOR TOWARD THE GATE THAT WOULD LEAD TO MY FREEDOM, I KNEW IF I DIDN'T LEAVE MY BITTERNESS AND HATRED BEHIND, I'D STILL BE IN PRISON.
>
> NELSON MANDELA

Your Choice

Throughout this book, you have been working on your story. I do not know if you have reached your parking lot moment yet. You still might not be ready to make the decision to let it all go.

You have released your control and deep disappointment. You have learned many things from your experience and your forgiveness journey.

I feel like I should light fireworks and bake you a cake to celebrate.

Why? Because forgiveness is a big deal! People spend a lifetime holding onto anger, pain, and unfulfilled expectations leading to piles of un-forgiveness that overshadow their lives.

FORGIVENESS IS THE LINK TO BRING BACK JOY!

Forgiveness is a decision you can make in a blink of an eye. Or gradually as you worked through your irreplaceable personal story. Either way, you are in a better place. I hope forgiveness has given you back some joy.

I marvel at people who have forgiven situations that are the size of mountains. Years ago, on separate occasions, I worked with two doctors who suffered huge tragedies. Both experienced the murder of their child. One child was only 12 years old, and he was shot after a mentally ill man broke into their home. The other was a beautiful young woman who was murdered by the notorious I-5 serial killer in 1982. In both cases, I learned a great deal as I watched the doctors navigate grief and loss through violent circumstances.

Both doctors helped so many people to get better. They listened intently as people poured out their own physical and mental pain. These patients had been unaware of the tragedy the doctors had undergone. Did the doctors forgive the murderers? That is not a question for me to answer. That is for each of them. As I have stated before, forgiveness takes place in their hearts. I can only tell you what I observed. Each of the doctors made a choice to move forward in their lives and make the world a better place.

Throughout history, people have sustained great pain because of what other individuals or societies have done. Each person has to decide how he or she will deal with the rage, heartache, and the desire for revenge they feel in their hearts.

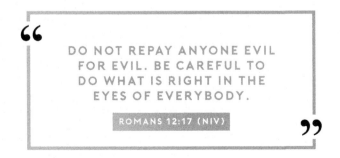

> **DO NOT REPAY ANYONE EVIL FOR EVIL. BE CAREFUL TO DO WHAT IS RIGHT IN THE EYES OF EVERYBODY.**
>
> ROMANS 12:17 (NIV)

In our society, we hook revenge to karma, and call it "payback." But revenge is not an avenue for healing. There are people who have gone through great agony because of another person's actions, and did not choose to get personal revenge. God has given us the avenue for human justice and the power to establish healthy boundaries. God is in charge of judging souls.

Clearly, evil for evil is not a good idea. When we are in pain, we want to give back what we got and add a dash more for good measure. That is not what God is asking for. What God wants you to do is to follow the laws of judicial justice. And in the case of unhealthy relationships, use the power of healthy boundaries. God wants you to be the light that comes from the dark.

What is everyday revenge? Is revenge an eye for an eye? Not always! We have all tried to get revenge at some point in our lives. We use terms such as, "they need to learn a lesson" or, "payback is a bitch." We justify doing or not doing something for someone because of hurt they have caused us. Even if we do this in a small way, it is still revenge in our hearts.

A Quick Revenge Story - Joy

Our mother is a powerful force in our lives. A mother-daughter relationship is especially filled with expectations from both sides. Some people are very lucky, and their relationship with their mother is everything they expected it to be. For the rest of us, we have to work on our expectations.

I was working with Joy, a successful, married woman, and a mother herself. She had long-standing issues leftover from her childhood, and unfulfilled expectations in her relationship with her mother. From the outside, her relationship with her mother looked good. They visited each other, spent holidays together, and talked on the phone a few times a week. But, looks can be deceiving.

Her mother had a long-standing problem with over-promising and under-delivering. As a child, her mom would forget the simple things from school supplies to leaving her at school. She learned early that she could not believe what her mom said she would do. As an adult, this pattern continued. It could be something as small as forgetting to send a gift for her grandson, to not picking her and her husband up at the airport as promised. Her daughter would have to prompt, coax, and remind her mother to follow through on everything. Her daughter could not figure out why her mother continued this pattern, because she knew how angry and frustrating it made everyone.

On one occasion, her mother was scheduled to fly in for a visit and Joy said to me, "she can find her way to my house from the airport this time. Maybe she'll understand what it's like to not be there when you say you will." She did this to teach her mom a lesson.

She wanted her Mom to feel what she felt on so many occasions. She also wanted a little revenge. Was this little piece of revenge going to change her mom? No, and it was causing Joy to act differently than usual. She was reacting from her pain.

After she had spent time looking at the story of her mother's life, she could see clearly that her mother was not malicious. (Deep down she already knew this.) Her mother wanted to fulfill every promise she had ever made at the time she made them. Her mother was also the type of person that did not like letting people down, even though that is exactly what the over-promising did.

Joy wanted to let it go and enjoy spending time with her mother. She wanted to stop trying to mother her mother. By understanding her mother's flaws, she could choose to change her expectations and be grateful for all the marvelous things her mother brought to the relationship.

Joy changed her expectations of her mom and not because she made her mom take a 15-minute taxi ride to her house from the airport. That did not even cause her mom to get upset. But because Joy now understood more about who her mom is and that her actions are not some evil plot to cause her daughter pain. Joy's mom does not have the skill to implement things in her life the way some other people do.

Joy now reminds herself that she cannot ask her mom more then she is capable of giving. Joy also stopped trying to teach her mother a lesson. Today, she is more grateful for her mom and the many positive qualities that she does possess.

Forgiveness is about letting go of trying to control other people's behavior. Understanding the relationship for the good and bad helps you to keep your expectations in check, and find things to be grateful for. By trying to teach other a lesson, you are trying to control them and get some sweet revenge.

Healthy Guidelines and Boundaries

I have mentioned healthy boundaries more than a few times as you have worked through this book. I want you to dig deeper and discover how boundaries can be another tool in your life to lead to less conflict and more forgiveness.

Healthy boundaries are the fences in our life. These fences prevent us from falling off the cliff, hurting ourselves and hurting others. These fences are not there to keep people out of our lives, but to allow them access through the gates we control. Being your own gatekeeper lets you be the best you. Boundaries are where our morals meet our actions. Those actions make a big difference in the quality of our lives and the lives of those around us.

Forgiveness gives you another choice to use the power of healthy boundaries. Boundaries are just one more link in the forgiveness chain. Messy lives entangled in pain cause people to turn their feelings into actions. Sometimes those actions can look needy, emotionally abusive, or even violent. It is your decision whether you let that overflow into your life, or create a healthy boundary.

We choose to be around people by the way they make us feel. So why should you put yourself around people who make you feel anxious, angry, hurt, or put you in physical danger? I can honestly say, I have placed myself in more than one of these situations. I stayed there for longer than I should have. It is always easier to see other people's circumstances and ask why they stay, then to ask ourselves why we do the same.

When you are with someone, you should feel happy, loved, accepted, and safe. It gets tricky when we love someone or have obligations to the people who are exhibiting dangerous behavior in our lives. Nothing is harder than having to draw lines in your life from a husband, son, daughter, or other close relatives or friends.

Forgiveness enables you to let go of the pain by changing your perspective of the story. Boundaries lets you have the ability to love from afar. It's the hands-off policy of forgiveness and boundaries.

I am sure the term "healthy boundaries" came about in a twentieth-century psychotherapy session to help someone get out of an uncomfortable situation or out of a bad relationship. However, the idea of healthy boundaries is not a new one. You can find instructions on healthy relationships in all of the Holy Scriptures from around the world. Do you think the great sages and prophets were not faced with crazy relatives? What do you bet Jesus had a second cousin or a grumpy uncle that made him not want to attend a family BBQ? Adam and Eve had two kids who caused serious family drama. Cain killed his brother because he was angry and jealous, causing the first murder in the Bible and the first heartbroken family. Even if you are relatives, that does not mean you should put yourself in an unhealthy setting.

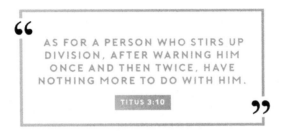

AS FOR A PERSON WHO STIRS UP DIVISION, AFTER WARNING HIM ONCE AND THEN TWICE, HAVE NOTHING MORE TO DO WITH HIM.

TITUS 3:10

Healthy Guidelines for Relationships

To have balance, you need to plan. You need to include well thought out parameters in your life. I have listed a few below, and you can add your own as well.

- Feeling respected for who you are; not for what you can do or give.
- Feeling safe; physically, emotionally, and mentally with the people in your life.
- Being able to express thoughts, emotions, and feelings without fear of judgment.
- The relationship is adding value to your life.
- Having a relationship with God, however that looks for you, so you can nurture your soul.

Your turn! What can you add as a healthy boundary to your life?

Giving Up Control

A very important concept about forgiveness (probably one of the hardest) is recognizing that we cannot control other people. I have tried and failed, have you?

Most of the time our need to control others is because we think that they could be and do better. If they are old enough to vote, it is up to them to make decisions for their lives. If your adult children, a relative, or a close friend makes bad decisions, you can only intervene as much as it is healthy for you. You can still love them, and pray for them (this is possibly the most powerful thing you can do), and, most importantly, you can still be kind.

Your forgiveness radar should be going off when you find yourself trying to control someone's negative behavior. For example, if you have forgiven your uncle for being a drunken good-for-nothing at every family holiday, and on the next holiday your uncle gets drunk again, do you have the right to be upset at him, again? Nope.

Forgiveness does not mean you are waiting for other people to change. In the case of the difficult loved one, you knew their struggles and what they are like. Yet, you chose to walk right back in. Is it okay that people behave badly? No, but that is not in question. Along with forgiving, you need to set healthy boundaries about interacting with people knowing that you are not in charge of trying to change them.

What if other people do not like the boundaries you have set for your life? You are over the age of eighteen and can make your own decisions. Yes, even if they upset other people who have no issues being around badly behaved people. If you do not want that behavior in your life, then stay away from it. You can communicate your boundaries in a kind, loving manner.

Love someone, but with distance. Remember the statement, "I wouldn't touch that with a 10-foot pole?" Sometimes you need to stay out of other people's lives because it causes you too much pain, anger, and un-forgiveness. That can be hard when it is a person you love.

Just because you forgive someone doesn't mean it is safe for you to have him or her in your life mentally, emotionally, or physically. You need to be honest about your fences, not try to control others, while still being kind. Each of us needs to keep an imagined 10-foot pole as a tool in our boundaries toolbox.

How Much Can We Help?

We all have our own stuff to carry. We are responsible for taking care of our own lives. At the same time, we need to lend a helping hand to our loved ones, neighbors, and those in need. Isn't that part of the reason we are here? But then the question becomes, to what level?

We all know people who will give up every last minute of their day or every last dime in their bank account to the relative who has gone down a destructive path. Have you ever tried to save a friend or family member who says they will do better next time? Only to descend into their negative, unhealthy choices again? Soon after, they return to you begging to be rescued with no real regard for your needs. It is terribly disappointing to see them crash and burn repeatedly. But you do not have to go down with them.

If you keep trying to rescue them, all the while forfeiting your wellbeing, you have now caused two people to be in trouble. God does not want you emotionally or financially ruined while you help others. You can help more people and situations if you are not a victim. You will still be called on to help your fellow man, but not to the destruction of yourself. Healthy boundaries will be the relief you need.

Taking Care of Yourself

Jesus is a good example of taking care of himself as he helped others. He was not able to help everyone. He did what he could, and then he had to move on. Jesus walked in nature. He took the time to breathe, rest, pray, and recharge. Jesus spent his time with friends and family who believed in him. He had twelve very close friends who lifted him up, cared about him, and supported his decisions. Buddha practiced right mindfulness. Understanding that our thoughts and actions determine what type of life we will have.

What are you doing to keep yourself mentally healthy? Are you doing similar things to Jesus and Buddha? Or are you spending your day so busy taking care of others that your mind has no time to rest and recharge? Is your spirit getting filled up? Do you find a place to see God? In church? In nature? In community service? Do you take the time to sit and read sacred scripture? There are so many things you can do to boost your battery power.

Part of having healthy boundaries is making sure you keep a certain degree of balance in your life. Americans are so obsessed with physical exercise, but we forget to exercise our heart, mind, and soul. So, jump on the love train, fill your mind with knowledge, and feed your soul with prayer. Make yourself a priority.

Want for yourself what you would want for the person whom you love the most. You would want them to be physically, emotionally, and spiritually content. Want that for yourself.

Clear boundaries provide a time management tool so your life can be filled with the things you choose, instead of the things which others choose for you. Because if you let them, they will choose. You can still honor your commitment to helping them. But honor them in a more thoughtful way that does not drain your emotional and physical tank.

You can also make a choice not to freak out when a crisis hits because you have already prepared the "boundaries" for when someone needs you. You have made your priorities, which fall into line with your values and morals. There are only so many hours in the day. Setting limits allows you be mindful of your life and the lives around you. Know yourself and your trigger points. If you know that you want to volunteer every month, then you will make that a priority and protect that time.

Learn from your past situations. Make new rules for yourself. For example, "I do not loan money to friends and family." You might make this rule because in the past when you have loaned money to friends and family, it has caused you hurt feeling and issues with un-forgiveness when they do not pay it back. If this is a hard and fast rule across the board, then you will no longer have to feel bad about loaning money to one person and not the other. Other examples can range from, "I do not loan my car to anyone that does not live in my house." "I will not bail you out of jail." (You may laugh, but I have had that jail request a few times.) Whatever your boundary is, it is yours, and other people do not have to like it or agree with it. In the same way, other people have free choice to set boundaries that work for their lives.

Clear and healthy boundaries must be established inside your home. When I was young, my parents made a rule that we were never allowed to say or call each other "stupid." My parents yelled, screamed, and threw things at each other, but they never called each other "stupid." My parent's boundaries did not make sense regarding their relentless chaotic behavior. As a child, I could not count on life having boundaries that kept me safe. Sure, I could count on the one rule about the word "stupid." However, I needed real boundaries in our family.

I keep the "stupid" rule as a boundary in my home today. I have also added a few additional well thought out boundaries that help keep my home a loving place. What is acceptable, and what is unacceptable in your home?

Think about the boundaries and rules in your life. Are you surrounding yourself with people who lift you up and support you? Do you have a healthy lifestyle for your body and mind? Is your home your sanctuary where you feel safe and loved?

Rules and boundaries are intentional. You decide on each and every rule to help make your life less complicated and more joyful. You have the power to design your life, so let's get designing.

What Will You Give?

Why you choose to give is equally as important as why you choose not to give. Think about what you want to give in your life. How much time do you want to give to your friends, family, and your career? How much money do you donate to charities and what charities do you choose? When it comes to boundaries with your family, friends, and strangers, you should have these mapped out before you put yourself in an uncomfortable position. Sit down with your spouse or immediate family and decide what those healthy family boundaries look like. Here are a few questions to ask yourself/spouse/family on the boundaries you would like to set.

- Do you want your relatives staying three days or two weeks? What is your limit?
- Do you loan money to friends or family?
- Is giving a percentage of your income part of your faith?
- How much money do you give?
- Do you give to charity, and if so, what charity do you choose?
- Do you give money on a regular basis?

- Do you volunteer your time?
- Will your giving grow with your income?
- How much time do you spend with family, and how much time do you spend with friends?
- What will you do for your career goals? (Move, work over time, take work home?)

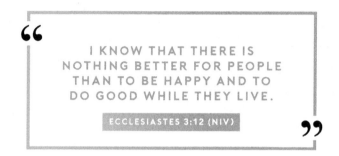

> **I KNOW THAT THERE IS NOTHING BETTER FOR PEOPLE THAN TO BE HAPPY AND TO DO GOOD WHILE THEY LIVE.**
>
> ECCLESIASTES 3:12 (NIV)

The Moral of Your Story

You can now put action into your future. You can now make decisions that involve a dose of extra wisdom you have gained on your journey. I feel like I should be singing, "You can see clearly now the rain is gone! Let the sunshine in." Don't worry; I won't sing. That would not be good for anyone. But go ahead and do a little dance, because you have learned so much. Your story is remarkable and unique.

Now that you have forgiveness as a tool, you have unlimited potential for an abundant life. God wants you to have a joyful life. I want that for you also.

Every good story has a moral, which teaches us something. In all the forgiveness stories you have read in this book, they have all learned deep life lessons. Forgiveness shifted the story from a never-ending cycle of pain to moving on and letting go.

Here is a story about Jodi and her journey from victim to victor with the help of gratefulness and forgiveness.

Jodi's Forgiveness Story

Jodi had worked in real estate for twenty years, so she knew how a real estate office functioned. She had managed agents and staff from little offices with three or four agents, to her current position. Jodi now organized and juggled the needs of thirty agents and their staff. Jodi had been working at her current office for eight years. She loved the profession and was highly respected. She could organize everything from human resources to scheduling staff education. She loved her job, even with the challenges that came with working alongside so many different personalities.

The head broker of the agency had recently gotten married and decided his new wife should also work in the office. The new wife would not only work for the head broker, but she would oversee the corporate operation. The new wife-employee was not on the payroll, and the only title she held was "Broker's Wife." Her authority was given, not earned, and it put Jodi in direct opposition.

With an office of this size, procedures and operations were always changing. Each agent had an assistant to help manage all the calls, paperwork, and clients. But in real estate, agents must have a head broker. The broker must have a broker's license to own his company. Real estate agents typically pay a percentage of their commission to the broker that they work for.

Jodi's job was to make sure everyone and everything flowed smoothly in a happy office environment. All the while ensuring that the agents and broker were compliant to the laws of real estate transactions. The wife had not run a real estate office, nor did she have Jodi's years of experience.

It was apparent almost immediately that this new addition had ideas that would cause Jodi serious drama. The wife would set up office meetings with agents and their assistants, never inviting Jodi. Then Jodi was required to do or change whatever had been decided on in the meetings. After the wife had hired a new person to handle Human Resources, Jodi tried to stand her ground both on principal and on the law. Jodi sat down with the head broker to express her concerns and her fears. She mistakenly hoped that reason would prevail. The wife dug in her heels, and she now had a target; Jodi. She wanted Jodi gone.

Soon Jodi had some of her tasks taken away, and she was banned from talking to the staff in fear that she would undermine the wife. This left Jodi feeling alienated, with nowhere to turn.

Jodi was experiencing extreme stress, and it showed in every part of her life. She gained weight, she could not sleep, and she now had hypertension. Jodi found that she was crying all the time and a sense of dread came over her every workday morning. At one point, she had daily anxiety attacks that caused immense, impending doom that made her feel like she could not breathe. At times the panic was so bad that her stomach clenched up causing her to vomit. She cannot remember a time when her life felt so out of control.

The stress of her work situation then seeped into her family life. Jodi's personal life was filled with love from her wonderful husband and two boys. But her family could see the toll her job was taking. Finally, on a Friday afternoon, the head broker called her into his office. He told her she was fired and she would receive two months of severance pay. Jodi did not know if she would accept it. If she did, did that mean that they were right and she was wrong? She had never been fired from any job and not fighting the mistreatment and unfairness felt like she would be saying that it was okay that this happened to her. It was not okay, and she wanted the people who had hurt her to know that.

Jodi called an attorney who advised her that this fight would take time, money and a lot more emotional stress. Jodi was already as stressed as her body and mind could take. Ultimately, she accepted the severance, still feeling every negative emotion: anger, pain, and betrayal. And now she felt like they had won.

Jodi's journey to forgiveness started when she saw a psychologist for the depression and anxiety caused by everything she had gone through. Being able to discuss the situation was very helpful. The psychologist told her that to forgive does not mean to forget. She was not going to forget everything that had happened to her, but she could forgive the people by looking at the situation as a debt. This debt was not money, but feelings. Those feelings of anger, pain, and betrayal, were not going to be compensated by the people who had hurt her. "How they did me wrong" was not going to be validated from the people Jodi wanted acknowledgment from. Knowing she was not going to be paid back for the emotional pain, Jodi started to realize that she was going to have to forgive the debt herself so that she could move on. Jodi easily found another job and the environment in her new office was calm and loving.

Even with the visit to the psychologist, Jodi still held onto the injustice and pain of her last situation. She still looked for details on the company, secretly hoping that they were not doing well. Her mind and heart still wanted an "I am sorry." Her heart still wanted the people who had caused *her so much pain to feel the pain she felt. She still carried un-forgiveness.*

Years later, Jodi found the Forgiveness Algorithm. Using the algorithm, Jodi wrote down her story and examined the story more closely to uncover some new information. She had held the story in her heart and head for so long, she was stuck on certain facts and overlooked others. Jodi now had a new perspective on the situation. Jodi's reaction to the situation had made her act in an unloving way, which was not normal for her. When we experience deep pain, it is common that we change our behavior. Jodi felt a deep sense of betrayal after being loyal to the company for eleven years.

Whether you are married, in a friendship, or in a work environment, you have formed relationships. If you invest your time and heart, it hurts when you feel you are no longer valued.

As Jodi went through the algorithm, she realized her actions did not reveal her best self. She was still hoping the people who had hurt her would get their punishment. Even though she had a great new job, she was letting her mind and heart return to the old painful situation, and hope that when they did fail, they would wake up and realize the wrong they did, and then she would get paid back on her emotional debt.

Jodi had done part of the work on her forgiveness journey. Seeing the therapist was very helpful, but she needed to let go. Examining the story, understanding what forgiveness is and what it is not, and doing more personal work, helped her to make the decision to forgive fully. After making that decision, Jodi accepted the situation and changed her perspective. She has not forgotten the pain she went through, but she remembers with new memories. The bonus to forgiving the people who had hurt her was that she now felt even more grateful for her new job. Her heart was now full.

Forgiveness is a transition out of being a victim to a victor, and from anger to gratefulness. The gratefulness can come from knowing you survived, you learned, and you are grateful for the people and situations that now bring you joy.

Forgiveness is an adventure full of waves of emotions and rocky relationships, leaving you with your story. It is time to find out what the moral of your story is.

WORK IT QUESTIONS

1. What did you learn about yourself during this forgiveness adventure?

2. Are you grateful for any part of this forgiveness experience? If so, what?

3. How will forgiving this person or situation help you in other un-forgiveness situations?

4. Has forgiveness changed your relationship? Or is this a relationship you should let go of?

5. Do you have a need for self-forgiveness?

6. Did you have any spiritual growth because of this forgiveness experience?

7. Are there boundaries you need to change or add to your life?

YOUR THOUGHTS:

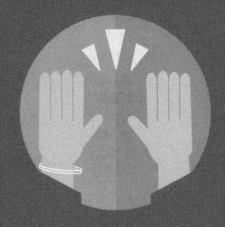

CELEBRATE!
CHAPTER NINE

STEP 5 - Celebrate
Forgiveness as a Lifelong Tool

You have done so much in our time together. You have soaked up so much information about forgiveness and worked your way through *Rev. Misty's Forgiveness Algorithm™* process. Way to go!

Rev. Misty's Forgiveness Algorithm™ is now a tool you can use, and use often. Practice, and practice some more. Recognize when you choose to pick up those un-forgiveness feelings because of another person's actions. Be aware of your forgiveness radar when you are feeling the urge to try to control another person's behavior. Be kinder to yourself. Forgive yourself for making poor choices learn and move on.

We all experience pain. Have you met one person in your life that does not have a story about pain? You cannot be a human being and not have pain in your life. If you grew up in a giant glass bubble where no one could hurt you, you would still be crying over some inner torture. None of us is born or die without experiencing emotional pain. The fact that you have experienced pain helps you be empathic to others and their pain. People who have grief help others with grief. People who have suffered tragedy help others who have suffered tragedy.

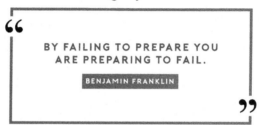

> **"**
> ### BY FAILING TO PREPARE YOU ARE PREPARING TO FAIL.
> BENJAMIN FRANKLIN
> **"**

The Bright Future Ahead

Now let's plan for a brighter future. In the same way, you used ceremony and intention to forgive a past hurt, you can use ceremony and intention to plan your future. Let's plan and prepare to have a joy filled life.

Write It, Say It, See It!

Where to start? Write it down, of course! Again, write yourself honest. What do you want? Be bold, be fearless, be adventurous!

Do you want to travel? Do you want new love in your life? What do you want when it comes to your career? Be fearless and think outside the box, plus have some fun with this exercise. Do not think about how things will happen, just write down your hopes and dreams for the future. Now you are telling the universe what you want, and you are opening your mind and heart to all the possibilities.

Write It Exercise

Answer these questions as you write down what you want your life to look like. Who do you want in your life? What will your relationship with your friends, family, or significant other look like? Be specific! For example, I want to spend time with my friends, laughing and eating great food. I want to have great adventures and travel. I want to go to Italy. Don't forget to put in some healthy boundaries.

Write down what you want in your career. What does it look like? Is your career your passion? Or do you want to change careers? Write everything down, including how much you get paid for what you do. One million dollars? Yes, you are worth it. If your chosen career pay range is not a million dollars, then pick a number that works for you.

What do you want in your spiritual life? Do you want to be more connected to God? Do you want to give back? How do you want that to look?

Okay, all the wonderful things you want in your life are now written down. Let's do more to help you activate the plan. You have written what you what, so now let's speak it. Read aloud what you have written and let God and your angels hear you. Turn your wishes into a prayer or a meditation. We are given free will, and spirit waits for us to ask for assistance. Let's ask God, our Angels, and Saints for assistance in our life.

Speak It Exercise

This is where you turn your wants into a prayer. Center yourself and take a deep breath. Feel your connection to God, the Angels, and all who love you. Start your prayer by being thankful for all that you have now, and for all that you are, because God made you to be amazing.

Pray with intent. Say what you mean and mean what you say. Explain to God and the Angels what you want for your life. Feel it in your heart and pray what you feel. How do you want your every day to be filled up? Be specific, leave out the fluff, and do not whine or complain. You are explaining to God your hopes, dreams, and desires.

Close your prayer as you opened it, with gratitude and love, thanking God for the blessings in your life. Close the prayer with "Amen." Amen

is not a "goodbye" or a "see you later." It has a much deeper meaning. When you say Amen at the end of a prayer, you are affirming your prayer. The definition of Amen is, "so be it." You are saying, "YES, it is." It is like taking a victory lap, arms in the air while yelling out, "So be it!"

Let it go! This is another place to let go. This time you are letting go of worry about what is next. You just handed it over to God.

Make prayer a habit. If you only pray in times of a crisis, it is like only hearing from a friend when they need something. Pray in both the good times and the bad. Say "Hi," to God. Have a personal relationship with God, not only a holiday relationship.

I have a friend who prays every morning before she gets out of bed. It is as important to her as getting in her physical exercise. Prayer in the morning sets the tone for your day. Make a habit and exercise your prayer muscle.

You have written down your desired future, you have spoken what you need and would like for your future, and now it is time to see it. A great practice is vision boarding, a creative way to see your life. You can keep your vision board at your desk or hang it on a bathroom wall. Every time you see it, it will remind you that you have a bright future full of possibilities.

See It Exercise

How do you envision your future?

Vision Board

Vision boarding is a creative way to map out your life. You can use a vision board as a compass to guide you on your way to your best life. You can use something as simple as poster board, magazines, photos or hand drawing. You can even make one virtually on your computer screen. Just make sure you put it somewhere you can see it each day.

Before you start, center yourself by meditation or prayer. The goal is to get to your sacred place, deep in your heart where your dreams rest. Then you are ready to start your vision board.

When you begin to think about what you want on your vision board, it is important that you do not let the roadblocks of fear stop you from envisioning your dreams. If your dream is to run a marathon, even though you cannot run a mile now, put a picture of a marathon runner crossing the finish line on your board. If your hearts aspiration is to travel and explore the world, add pictures of the countries you want to visit. You can also place words on your vision board, (i.e. peace, love, friendship, family, harmony) which reflect what you want in your personal, family, or work relationships. Think big and without boundaries. Imagine what it would feel like to accomplish goals and have the relationships your heart longs for. Make or change your vision board anytime you are in a transition in your life.

When you see where you want to go, you can start to put action in your life to get there. Your vision board is an external expression of your internal hearts desires. You can also use it as a prayer tool. Reminding you to add your long-term goals and relationships to your prayer life. Ultimately, bringing gratefulness into your life when something on your vision board is completed.

“ THE GOAL OF A VISION BOARD EXERCISE IS TO REFRAME YOUR CURRENT AND FUTURE SELF.

REV. LAURIE DEL PINO ”

Creating a Life Vision Statement

Before I was a reverend, my career was in large corporations. Each corporation had a vision statement that focuses everyone on how the corporation will act or grow. A life vision statement does the same thing. It can be the guiding theme for your life.

A life vision statement should align with your beliefs and how you want to conduct yourself in the future. They are usually short and to the point. You should make it short enough so you can memorize it. My life's vision statement is so important to me that I used it for my personal vows during my ordination. It reminds me of my deep desire to follow God and how I want to live my life.

Here are some examples of Life Vision Statements:
- I will live an authentic, adventurous, spiritual life while being devoted to my friends and family.
- My vision for my life is to create, nurture and maintain loving relationships.
- The vision for my life is to improve the world by making daily choices that help heal others and nurture my heart.
- In my life, I choose to honor the indwelling of God in my soul with my actions and decisions.

When you have your life's vision statement, it can be a tool for you to use when making decisions. Because your vision statement reflects how you want your life to look, it can quickly help you choose a course of action that is in-line with your beliefs.

Now it is your our turn to write your life's vision statement.

Thank You, Thank You!

Wow, you are at the end of our journey. Your feet are on dry land and you are holding the paddle above your head in victory! You have looked back so that you can move forward.

Life will keep moving and advancing; time stops for no one. It will be full of obstacles, hardships, and lessons. Therefore, this will not be your last forgiveness journey. But never forget, you hold power. The power of forgiveness! With this power, you can shape your life so that you will have more joy, peace, and happiness. Most importantly, remember God is with you, and God is Love.

It is an honor that you chose to use the *Rev. Misty's Forgiveness Algorithm* ™ to map out your journey. I know using forgiveness will help make your life happier. Forgiveness is the link between love and healing!

Final Worksheet

Forgiveness is a lifetime exercise. I have added a quick worksheet that you can go to when you find yourself in an un-forgiveness situation.

What or Who do you want to forgive?

CONSTRUCT **YOUR STORY**

In a page or less, construct your story and events that caused you un-forgiveness.

EXAMINE **THE STORY**

What were your expectations that were unfulfilled?

Do you feel loss over the person or situation?

What part of the situation do you take responsibility for?

Do you need to apologize?

WHAT DO YOU NEED TO PREPARE

FOR YOUR FORGIVENESS JOURNEY?

What can you do to help yourself heal?
Use your Tool Box. (Therapy, Journaling, Spiritual Guidance, Prayer, Reading, Dialogue, Ceremony, Time)

FORGIVE   IT'S YOUR CHOICE!

Breathe deep and make the decision. You must say YES or NO!

FORGIVENESS...

...IS YOUR CHOICE	...IS NOT FORGETTING
...IS A DECISION TO STOP TRYING TO CONTROL A PERSON OR A SITUATION	...IS NOT SAYING WHAT HAPPENED WAS OKAY
...IS TAKING RESPONSIBILITY FOR YOUR ACTIONS AND MAKING AMENDS	...IS NOT LETTING THE PERSON OUT OF JUSTICE
...IS A LONELY BUSINESS (HAPPENS IN YOUR SOUL, HEART, + MIND ONLY)	...IS NOT LETTING THE PERSON OUT OF THE CONSEQUENCES
...IS HAVING HEALTHY BOUNDARIES	...IS NOT SAYING YOU WILL NO LONGER BE SAD OR WISH IT WERE DIFFERENT

Appendix

Grief

- *The Grief Recovery Handbook* by John W. James and Russell Friedman This is an incredible book that walks you through the landmines of grief and gives you the tools to move through it into recovery. The authors also touch on forgiveness. You can find local "Grief Recovery Method" support groups that use the handbook along with Certified Grief Recovery facilitators on their website, www.griefrecoverymethod.com.

Therapy

Psychologists are trained in the study of the mind and human behaviors. Counselors provide talk therapy. Psychiatrists are physicians who can prescribe medication for help with Schizophrenia, Bipolar, Depression, Attention Deficit Disorder, along with other mental health disorders.

Licensed Therapists
- LMFT or MFT Licensed Marriage and Family Therapist
- LMHC or MHC, Licensed Mental Health Counselor
- LPC Licensed Professional Counselor

Doctors
- Doctor of Psychology Psy.D. – Cannot prescribe medication.
- Psychiatrist – Medical doctor who has chosen to specialize in the disease of the mind – can prescribe medication.

Therapist Resources
- http://www.aamft.org

This site can help you find a marriage and family counselor in your area. Please check coverage with your insurance and also check references. Your health insurance company can give you a list of therapists and psychiatrists covered by your plan.

It is always good to check with friends and see who they have visited and if they have had good results. Nothing is better than getting a referral from someone that you trust. Your primary care physician can also give you list of therapists that they have referred to and have seen good results.

Life Coach Resources
- https://www.lifecoachhub.com/coach-directory
- http://www.wellness.com - This site has listings for most states. The site does not endorse or rate any practitioners on the site. Please check references.

Meditation
- Essential Oils https://doterra.com
  I found an essential oil blend called "Forgive" by the company Do'Terra. The scent is lovely. I would recommend this oil, or try a different one that feels good in your heart. Use a diffuser or you can dab a drop of the oil onto your skin. Check that the oil you choose is safe for your skin and dilute as needed. Use it during your meditation, before you sit down to pray, or in a ceremony similar to the candle.

Meditation Resources
- https://www.headspace.com
- http://www.tm.org
- http://christianmeditationroom.com
- If you want to meditate with your eyes open, a great company called Mind Power Technology is a perfect choice. You can find the "Forgiveness Solution©" session at MindPT.com, along with other personal development and self-improvement sessions.

Prayer
The power of prayer has been established in medical studies and authors have written extensively on the subject. If you would like to research prayer and healing, pick up the books listed below.
- *Healing Words: The Power of Prayer and the Practice of Medicine* by Larry Dossey
- *Spirituality in Patient Care: Why, Who, Where and What* by Harold G. Koenig, M.D.

And a study done in 2001 and published in a peer review journal:
- The Journal of Reproductive Medicine, Nov 2004, researchers investigated the impact of intercessory prayer on outcomes of in-vitro fertilization-embryo transfer.

If you would like to research new ways to pray, I recommend a few great books.

- *How to Pray*, by Celeste Yacoboni and Mirabai Starr
- *The Way We Pray: Celebrating Spirit* from Around the World by Maggie Oman Shannon.

One of my favorites is a very old (1535 AD) book, an essay Martin Luther wrote to his barber, who asked him, "How do you pray?"

- *A Simple Way to Pray* by German Monk Martin Luther

Thank you to the Fetzer Institute for permission to use their Love and Forgiveness Survey, 2010

***Unlikely Friends* Documentary**

Released in 2013 http://www.unlikelyfriendsforgive.com

Betty Tyme - mid 1960's

Glenn, Misty's Twin

Glenn and Misty, age 2

CPSIA information can be obtained
at www.ICGtesting.com
Printed in the USA
FSOW04n0507090617
34907FS